Tokyo

Front cover: Shinjuku Avenue at dusk

Right: modern-day geisha

Sumo More an art than a sport – watch the battles of the giants at the Kokugikan (page 90)

Asakusa Kannon Temple At the heart of Edo cultur (page 40)

City Hall Forty-five floors high, its two towers have magnificent views over the city (page 70)

Ginza Eye-popping façade and ultra-fashionable stor make it the top place to g shopping (page 38)

Tsukiji Fish Market Get up early to enjoy the best sushi breakfast (page 72)

Tokyo Skytree The city's newest tower is the second tallest structure in the world (page 46)

Meiji-jingu shrine Surrounded by tranquil woods, it is dedicated to Emperor Meiji, founder of modern Japan (page 65)

Mt Fuji Take a trip to Japan's most famous mountain (page 81)

Ukiyo-e Ota Memorial Museum of Art One of the finest private collections of ukiyo-e woodblock prints (page 68)

Imperial Palace Once part of Edo Castle, in its day it was the largest fortification in the world (page 27)

A PERFECT DAY

8.30am Breakfast

Perch at a window seat in one of the city's ubiquitous coffee shops for a ringside view of the world's most bustling rush hour. Any spot near a large train station in the central downtown area will do.

9.30am Fishy business

Poke around the stalls at the Tsukiji Central Wholesale Fish Market for a sneak peek of the daily catch before it heads to restaurants throughout Japan.

11.00am Artworks

For an art fix, check out the public sculptures at Ueno Park then, depending on your mood, head to the Tokyo National Museum or the National Museum of Western Art. If animals interest you more, drop into nearby Ueno Zoo.

1.00pm Elegant eating

Hop on the Yamanote Line to Hamamatsucho Station for lunch at the magnificent Tofuya Ukai (www.ukai.co.jp/english/shiba), right next to Tokyo Tower. It's a classic Japanese eatery serving multi-course *kaiseki* cuisine in private rooms that look out on to a tranquil garden.

2.30pm Shop time

The streets of nearby Ginza, with their upmarket boutiques and fashion houses, beckon for an afternoon stroll. The large department stores on the main Chuo Dori drag are the best places to start, but explore the side streets for lesser-known brands and one-off shops.

IN TOKYO

5.00pm **Sky-high sunset**

The 54-storey Mori Tower in Roppongi Hills boasts shops, restaurants, bars and a major art museum. But if you just want to laze around and enjoy the sunset, the panoramic windows on the top floor offer a 360-degree vista.

9.00pm **Karaoke**

The night is still young, and choices abound. Check out live blues at Aoyama's Blue Note or jazz at Roppongi's STB 139 club. If neither strikes the right chord, fear not – on just about every street corner you'll find karaoke rooms where you can be the star.

4.00pm **Afternoon tea**

Enjoy a classic afternoon tea service in the resplendent lobby lounge of the Ritz-Carlton Tokyo; for a more Japanese take on snack time, order green tea and traditional Japanese sweets at Toraya Akasaka Tea Room (4-9-22 Akasaka, Minato-ku).

7.00pm **Dinner bell**

Head back downstairs for steaks and martinis at the Oak Door in the Grand Hyatt Tokyo hotel. Or if sake and seafood are more to your taste, nearby Inakaya serves up both in a rollicking atmosphere.

CONTENTS

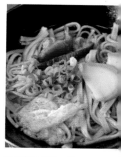

INTRODUCTION

Tokyo has earned a reputation as a fast-paced world capital, but what surprises many visitors is the calm that lurks in every corner of the city – the placid shrine sitting alongside the gleaming shopping mall, the tranquil precision of the tea ceremony, the hushed attention of reverent museum-goers. Tokyo offers an experience for everyone.

Geographically and demographically, this is one of the biggest cities in the world. Tokyo stretches 24km (15 miles) north to south and 88.5km (55 miles) east to west. The population of the 23 central wards alone is about 8.5 million. The best way for a visitor to make sense of all this is to divide the city into two areas, with Ginza, the Imperial Palace grounds and the Marunouchi financial quarter between them. On either side there are different topographies, and lifestyles as different from one another as night and day.

A City of Two Halves

Roughly to the east and north lies Shitamachi, an area of working-class neighbourhoods, ateliers and small factories clinging stubbornly to what remains of the traditional Tokyo way of life. That tradition is intensely communal: if you live in Shitamachi, you're likely to run into most of the people you know in the course of the day. Much of Shitamachi is horizontal – block after block of one-storey and two-storey wooden-frame houses and shops, many of them rebuilt just as they were before the fire bombings of 1945. The scale is eminently human. Everywhere in urban Japan the percentage of three-generation households gets smaller year by year. Nevertheless, in Shitamachi it is still quite common to live

Tokyo's cherry trees tend to blossom in early April

Small, family-owned shops can be found in Shitamachi

with one's parents and grandparents. Most of Tokyo's surviving public bathhouses are in Shitamachi. What more natural way to end the day than up to your neck in hot water alongside your friends and neighbours?

To the west and south – 'uptown' – is Yamanote, the Tokyo of boutiques and shopping arcades, swanky hotels and concert halls, embassies and government buildings, trendy restaurants and cafés. Life in Yamanote is as vertical as the building codes will allow. There are still a few pockets of single-family homes, but most people live, shop and work in high-rises. There are certain quarters of Yamanote, such as Shinjuku and Roppongi, that virtually never sleep: bars and discos are open until the first morning trains. If there's something new and different to be tasted in Tokyo – tapas bars, pet pampering parlours, DJ clubs – Yamanote is usually the first to offer it.

Tokyo rises to the task of moving its enormous population from place to place with a complex but extremely efficient public transport system that includes 14 subway lines, the Japan Railways (JR) Yamanote loop and Chuo crosstown lines, and 10 private railways that ferry commuters to and from the neighbouring prefectures of Kanagawa, Saitama and Chiba. Where the lines intersect are the city's commercial, cultural and entertainment centres: Ueno, Asakusa, Ginza, Roppongi, Shibuya, Harajuku and Shinjuku. At Shinjuku, where eight subway and railway systems converge, more than 3 million people pass through the station building every day.

Ever-Changing Style

Tokyo is a city of enormous creative and entrepreneurial energy, much of which goes into reinventing itself. Unlike the great capital cities of Europe, there is no prevailing style of architecture, no monumental core with which a new building might harmonise or clash. Even after the collapse of the economic bubble in 1992, the construction projects continued – and these days new buildings are sprouting everywhere on the Tokyo skyline. Whole blocks of the city seem to disappear overnight, replaced in the blink of an eye by new office buildings, condominiums, cultural complexes and shopping centres.

How Big is Tokyo?

Tokyo is far bigger than most people think. Like an onion, it has numerous layers. The inner city comprises 23 wards (ku), surrounded by dense suburbs and rural areas classified either as 'cities' (shi), towns (cho) or villages (son). These merge almost imperceptibly with the surrounding suburbia: Chiba to the east (almost as far as Narita Airport), Saitama to the north and Kanagawa (including Kawasaki and Yokohama) to the south. This untrammelled sprawl forms the largest urban agglomeration in the world, with an overall population of more than 33 million (over 26 percent of Japan's total). But there's more. The area administered by the Metropolitan Government stretches from the banks of the Sumida River to the mountains of Tanzawa and Oku-Tama far to the west. It also includes a chain of islands stretching south almost to the Tropic of Cancer, including the Izu chain, the Ogasawara group and the Iojima islets.

Nobody strolls in Tokyo. In fact, there are few places to sit down outdoors and watch the world go by. For a city that is known for embracing all kinds of cultural trends, the long, leisurely lunch hour has yet to catch on. People in Tokyo are always in a hurry to get somewhere.

Although the crime rate in Tokyo has risen significantly in recent years, it remains relatively low compared to most Western capitals. As a visitor you are unlikely to be the victim of a mugging or random act of violence. A network of small local police substations, known as *koban*, have helped to contain incidence of crime. On average, there's one *koban* for every 2 sq km (less than a square mile), and there are more in the shopping and nightlife areas. In each substation there are two or three officers on duty day and night. The Tokyo Metropolitan Police Department is a force some 41,000 strong, but you seldom see a patrol car in the city; instead, most officers are on the street. And since they know where everything is on their beat, you can always count on them when you've lost your way – as you're likely to do at least once in this complicated city.

Freedom to roam

Faced with a rapidly ageing population, Tokyo has adopted the buzzword 'barrier-free' – making buildings and infrastructure, such as street kerbs, subway platforms, station toilets and museum entrances, accessible to people in wheelchairs. With a few conspicuous exceptions, Tokyo is getting significantly friendlier to those with physical disabilities.

The Denizens of 'Downtown' Tokyo

Chances are that anyone you meet uptown in Tokyo was born and raised – or lives – elsewhere. Shitamachi, on the other hand, belongs to the Edokko: the people who can trace their local Tokyo roots back at least three generations. Gossipy, busy, openhearted, the Edokko have defined what it means to be 'from Tokyo' for more than

A wall of neon in Shinjuku

300 years. The Edokko are notoriously prodigal: saving might be a necessity, but it's no particular virtue.

The Edokko are also prone to sentimentality and to what they call *ninjo*: the web of small favours and kindnesses that bind them together. Sneeze in the middle of the night and your neighbour will demand the next morning that you take better care of yourself. Stay home with a fever and she will be over by noon with a bowl of soup. A shopkeeper will breathe a sigh of relief when his son – the fifth or sixth in the family line – finally decides to settle down and take over the business. An Edokko craftsman would rather lose a commission than take any criticism from a customer who doesn't know good work when he sees it.

The Edokko quarrel in a language all their own, an earthy local dialect. Ignore the proprieties, or offend the pride of an Edokko, and he will let you know about it in no uncertain terms. Respect his values and you make a friend for life.

Takeshita Street is the focal point of teenage culture in Harajuku

Capital of Cool

While the pulse of the old ways can still be felt among the Shitamachi backstreets, the future of Tokyo is being forged on the other side of town. The emergence of homegrown J-pop stars, new-media entrepreneurs, and *wunderkind* fashion designers has reshaped the city's image and given rise to the international phenomenon of 'Japan Cool'.

Theirs isn't the *Blade Runner* vision of Tokyo, with its giant video screens, talking vending machines, and gigantic signs flickering in neon *kanji* characters. Instead, the new generation has made its mark via animation studios, concert halls and fashion runways. And the government has taken notice – tax dollars are flowing in to promote the new vision of Tokyo at pop-culture festivals both at home and abroad. The new vibe can feel both exhilarating and disorienting – much like a visit to this enormous, remarkable city.

A BRIEF HISTORY

Until the 12th century, Tokyo (then called Edo) was an unimportant fishing village at the mouth of the Sumida River. In those days, the political and cultural life of Japan centred on the Heian imperial court in Kyoto. By 1185, however, the authority of the court had collapsed, and feudal warlords established a military government of their own (the *bakufu*, or shogunate), based in Kamakura, just south of present-day Tokyo. The Sumida River watered one of the few really extensive fertile plains in eastern Japan. This region eventually came under the sway of one of those warlords, Ota Dokan, who built the first castle in Edo in 1457. The event marked the beginning of Tokyo's rise to prominence.

Early Tokugawa Period

In the 16th century the feudal system that was consolidated under the Kamakura shogunate disintegrated into a period of civil war, known as the 'Age of the Warring States'. In 1590, Edo (and the eight surrounding provinces) passed into the hands of a warlord, Tokugawa Ieyasu. It was an enormous fortune; the earnings of his fief could theoretically have provided the annual living wage for 2.5 million people.

Ieyasu, however, had even grander ambitions: he wanted the whole country. In 1600, at the battle of Sekigahara, in the mountains of south-central Japan, he destroyed a coalition of his rivals, and established himself as ruler of the archipelago. He replaced Ota's castle with one of his own, vastly larger and stronger, and in 1603 made

'Mouth of the river'

Tokyo's original name Edo means 'mouth of the river'. It wasn't until 1869 that the name Tokyo, meaning 'eastern capital', was introduced by Emperor Meiji.

Tokugawa Ieyasu, founder of
the Tokugawa shogunate

Edo the official capital of the Tokugawa shogunate. When Ieyasu died in 1616, rule passed to his son. The imperial court remained in Kyoto, but it was only a marginal force in national affairs; the new seat of power in Edo was the undisputed centre. By 1720 the city had a population of over a million. It was larger, better administered and more sophisticated than any European capital of the age.

Much about present-day Tokyo can be traced to its days as a castle town. If the city seems confusing and difficult to navigate, it was meant to be just that way. Ieyasu had learned a thing or two about betrayal and self-preservation as he rose to power. Moats, towers and high stone walls were not enough to protect him; the whole city was his defence. Mazes of narrow, twisty streets made it difficult for anybody to move towards the centre in force.

For over 250 years, no one offered a serious military threat to the Tokugawa shogunate. The *daimyo* (lords) and their lesser retainers were never called out in defence of the capital, functioning instead as a civil service. Bureaucracy became the city's biggest industry and never left town. Decisions of state today are still made – and funded – in Tokyo, touching the everyday lives of the Japanese people in myriad, all-pervasive ways. Most of the lords' villas were in Yamanote, south and west of the castle, and some still survive today as parks, public gardens and hotel grounds.

Emergence of Edo Culture

For all its power, the Tokugawa bureaucracy was never more than a minority in Edo, but it generated most of the demand for goods and services. The city grew at an astonishing rate, as people were drawn here from all over the country to help provide the warrior class with food, clothing, furniture – and fun.

It was in the narrow streets and alleys in the eastern part of the city that true Edo culture was born. An old proverb asserts that whatever money the people here had in their pockets at nightfall would be gone by morning. They spent their money in the pleasure quarters, as well as on fireworks festivals, intricate stencil-dyed fabrics and kabuki, the dramatic art that emerged in the 17th century and 100 years later had become the 'people's theatre' *par excellence* (see page 84). And nowhere were the plays more lavish and spectacular, the actors more revered, and the audiences more enthusiastic than in Edo.

18th-century painting *Kabuki Entertainers*

Edokko also spent their money on *ukiyo-e* ('pictures of the floating world'), Japan's unique tradition of woodblock printing. The world-renowned masters of the art – Hokusai, Sharaku, Utamaro, Hiroshige – all worked in the Edo period, and the common people of the city bought their work in droves: pictures of actors and courtesans, landscapes, albums and greeting cards, sex manuals and illustrated books. The shogunate would try, from time to time, to rein in some of this exuberance, but to little effect. For those with funds, the pursuit of pleasure and diversion had become a way of life.

Fall of the Shogunate

The shogunate governed successfully for so long in part because there were no baneful outside influences to disturb the peace. The third Tokugawa shogun, Iemitsu, had declared the country closed to the world in 1639. With some minor exceptions, foreigners were forbidden to enter Japan and the Japanese

Dog Shogun

The first Tokugawa shogun, Ieyasu, unified the country and created his capital in Edo. The second and third extended and consolidated their hold on power. Of the 12 succeeding shoguns, few were of note, apart from the eccentric Tsunayoshi, the fifth head of the dynasty. He decreed the death sentence for anyone found to have killed a dog and ordered lavish shelters to be built around the city to house stray canines. Even so, the 'Dog Shogun', as he became known, was a reformer. Under his rule, Edo was transformed from a military base into a thriving city for commerce and the arts. The Genroku period (1688–1704) under his rule was a time of development of the urban culture and arts now thought of as typically Japanese: kabuki theatre; *ukiyo-e* woodblock prints; the 'floating world' of the Yoshiwara licensed quarter; connoisseurship of *sake* and *soba*; intricately dyed Edo-komon kimono; and the idea of Edokko (son of Edo).

were forbidden to leave. The exclusion policy came to an end in 1853 with the arrival of Commodore Matthew C. Perry, commanding a fleet of American warships and bearing the demand of the US government for a treaty that would open Japan's ports to international trade.

Commodore Perry, who ended Japanese isolation

The shogunate was by this time too weak to resist, and its resulting capitulation inspired a group of clans from the far southwestern part of the country to stage a coup d'état. They seized the Imperial Palace in Kyoto and demanded that the Tokugawa government step down; political power, they insisted, would revert to the imperial throne. There was a brief civil war, which ended in 1869 with the defeat of the shogun. Emperor Meiji moved his court to Edo from Kyoto and renamed it Tokyo – the 'eastern capital'.

Early 20th-Century Disasters

Through the late 19th and early 20th centuries, the city grew steadily larger and more important as the political and economic centre of an emerging modern state. It retained the broad general divisions into the districts of Yamanote (west and south) and Shitamachi (east and north), but grew vastly more complicated, adding sub-cities and commercial centres, expanding to the north and west, reclaiming land from Tokyo Bay and linking itself by rail to the neighbouring port of Yokohama.

Then disaster struck. At 11.58am on 1 September 1923, an earthquake that measured nearly 8 on the Richter scale

Firestorms

When the Great Kanto Earthquake occurred on 1 September 1923, it caused considerable damage. But far worse devastation was caused by the conflagration that ensued. Firestorms raged for 48 hours, leaving over 140,000 people dead or missing and almost 65 percent of homes in Tokyo destroyed.

hit the Tokyo area. The fires that broke out after the earthquake destroyed over half the city (see box). Tokyo rebuilt, but ignored the opportunity to change its shape; instead, the city grew back the way it had always been – an irrational composite of quarters and subcentres.

In the early 1930s the power of generals and admirals over the government increased and the country began to take a more militaristic path, with popular support from ultra-nationalist groups. Japan went on to invade China and ally itself with Nazi Germany and Fascist Italy. The US responded with a trade and fuel embargo, cutting off 90 percent of Japan's oil supplies. The result was the attack on the American fleet at Pearl Harbor (7 December 1941) and total war.

Japan had early successes, invading the Philippines, Borneo, Malaya, Singapore and the Dutch East Indies, but at the Battle of Midway in June 1942 the tide began to turn. In 1945 Tokyo was reduced to rubble. In a single night, 100,000 of its inhabitants were killed when American warplanes firebombed the city. On 15 August 1945 Japan surrendered and soon afterwards the occupation and reconstruction of the country began. In the immediate post-war period, mere rebuilding was as much as most people could handle. Ideas such as zoning and large-scale city planning were luxuries Tokyo couldn't afford.

Building of Modern Tokyo

The Allied occupation of Japan ended in 1952. Over the next decade, the country embarked on a period of economic growth, planned and directed by the central government. To be near the seats of power, the major banks, construction contractors and corporations needed to have locations in Tokyo. By 1960, the city's population had grown to 9.7 million.

The beginning of Japan's return to prominence in world affairs was marked by Tokyo's successful bid to host the 1964 Olympic Games. The city embarked on an orgy of building to produce the necessary infrastructure. The airport at Haneda was improved and linked to the city by monorail. The Tokaido Shinkansen high-speed rail network began whisking passengers between Tokyo and Osaka at speeds of 270km/h (168mph). The first sections of toll road opened on the Tokyo Metropolitan Express system, taking some of the burden of traffic from the city's congested streets. The Olympics gave the world a first taste of Japan's efficiency; visitors to Tokyo discovered a mega-city that really 'worked' – and still does.

A camera factory at the start of the 'Economic Miracle'

During the 1960s, Tokyo was the focal point for the Japanese 'Economic Miracle', a period in which the economy grew at a rate of about 10 percent a year, doubling the national income. Ambitious public works projects gave the city governmental and cultural landmarks such as the Supreme Court and the National Theatre. Huge high-rise housing developments like that of Takashima-daira in the northwest were astonishingly ugly, but they raised the stock of affordable apartments within commuting distance of the city centre.

The domestic market for cars more than quadrupled. The physical face of the city, the pace of life and the quality of the air all changed accordingly. Air pollution is now at far more tolerable levels, but traffic can still be maddening and an off-street parking space anywhere in the central wards can cost more than ¥50,000 a month.

The following decades were an enormously restive period for Tokyo. In 1968–9, the city was convulsed by violent student protests against the renewal of the United States–Japan Mutual Security Agreement. Longer and more violent was the opposition (by local residents and student radicals) to the new Tokyo international airport at Narita; construction began in 1969, but the protest movement delayed the actual opening of the airport until 1978.

Bursting of the Bubble

The 'Bubble Economy' of 1984–90 changed the face of Tokyo again, in ways far more extensive and profound than had the 'Miracle' of the 1960s. Speculation drove the price of land in the city far above even remotely realistic levels. Banks clamoured to lend on real estate; borrowers could demand and receive 125 percent or more of the value of their collateral. Tokyo went on a building binge: modest two-bedroom apartments in new high-rises on the Sumida waterfront – or in luxury city-within-a-city developments like Ebisu Garden Place

– were snapped up at million-dollar prices. Yen exchange rates and stock values skyrocketed out of sight, and the Japanese embarked on buying sprees around the world.

The symbolic events in this boom were the removal of the Tokyo Metropolitan Government offices from Marunouchi to West Shinjuku in 1991, and the construction on their previous site of the Tokyo International Forum conference complex. Both of these monumental, spare-no-expense projects trumpeted Tokyo's pride in its newfound wealth and power.

Then the bubble burst. Real-estate prices started falling in 1992, a trend that continued for over a decade, and the stock market followed suit, leaving the corporate sector saddled with debt. Bankruptcy and long-overdue corporate restructuring put thousands of people out of work, swelling the ranks of the homeless and the encampments of cardboard and blue tarpaulin shelters around the city.

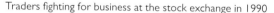

Traders fighting for business at the stock exchange in 1990

Reinvention

The 'Heisei Recession' lasted well into the new millennium, but in central Tokyo it was hard to find evidence of slowdown, as building projects continued unabated. Roppongi Hills, with its massive central tower, was the most visible of these projects, but elsewhere the skyline has been transformed. Virtually every building in Marunouchi, the business district in front of Tokyo Station, has been revamped or redeveloped, mostly vertically. The old Shiodome freight yard between Shinbashi and the bay has sprouted skyscrapers, as has the Shinagawa InterCity project. In Nihonbashi, the 2005 Mitsui Tower has reinvigorated one of Tokyo's most traditional areas. And back in Roppongi is a second huge tower, the Midtown Project.

In 2011 disaster struck again, only this time it wasn't man-made. The earthquake that devastated northeast Japan on 11 March did not cause extensive damage in Tokyo, but its impact was felt in other ways – in the stream of evacuees entering the city, in the deepening of the economic recession, in the surge of massive anti-nuclear protests. It wasn't long, though, before residents returned to shops, restaurants and department stores (thanks in large part to promotions benefiting stricken areas), and when the world's second tallest tower, Tokyo Skytree, debuted a year later, the city – and the nation – had begun to heal in earnest.

The Swiss architects Herzog and de Meuron designed Prada's Tokyo shop

It is this dynamism and urge to reinvent an entire cityscape that has and will continue to characterise Tokyo as one of the world's great metropolises.

Historical Landmarks

1457 Warlord Ota Dokan fortifies hill overlooking Edo (Tokyo) Bay.

1600–3 Tokugawa shogunate founded, with Edo as its capital.

1657 Fire destroys 70 percent of the city.

1688–1704 The Genroku period under the fifth shogun, Tsunayoshi, sees the flowering of Edo culture.

1703 The 47 Ronin Incident. The killing of a senior shogunate official by a band of avenging samurai inspires a popular kabuki play.

1707 Mt Fuji erupts for the last time.

1853 Commodore Perry leads fleet of US ships into Edo Bay.

1868–9 Emperor Meiji overthrows Tokugawa shogunate, gives Edo the new name 'Tokyo'.

1894 Japan wins Sino-Japanese War, takes Taiwan.

1905 Japan defeats Russia in the Russo-Japanese War.

1912 Emperor Meiji dies. Under Emperor Taisho, Japan enjoys a brief period of liberal parliamentary democracy.

1923 The Great Kanto Earthquake leaves over 140,000 dead or missing.

1926 Emperor Taisho dies. Emperor Showa (Hirohito) accedes.

1937 The Marco Polo Bridge Incident triggers an invasion of China, the precursor to Japan's involvement in World War II.

1940 Japan signs Tripartite Axis.

1945 Tokyo suffers extensive damage in US firebombing raids. Japan surrenders after atomic bombing of Hiroshima and Nagasaki.

1945–52 Allied occupation of Japan, with Tokyo as headquarters.

1960s The 'Economic Miracle' transforms the city.

1964 Tokyo hosts the Summer Olympic Games.

1968–9 Protests over US-Japan Security Treaty.

1989 Emperor Showa dies; start of the Heisei era.

1991 Metropolitan Government offices move to West Shinjuku.

1995 Fatal sarin gas attack on the Tokyo subway.

1995–9 Japan enters recession and restructures its economy.

2011 The Great East Japan Earthquake kills 17,000 people and sparks a nuclear crisis.

WHERE TO GO

Although Tokyo is one of the world's largest, most complicated and densely populated cities, the first-time visitor can easily find the most interesting neighbourhoods and sights. We start our tour with some of the oldest districts, continue on to the nerve centres of modern Tokyo and finish with a few highlights of trips to nearby attractions outside the city.

THE IMPERIAL PALACE AND ENVIRONS

Go to the heart of things and begin your sightseeing at the **Imperial Palace ❶** (Kokyo). The palace grounds are what remain of Edo Castle, which in Tokugawa Ieyasu's day was the largest, most complex system of fortifications in the world. The outer perimeter was a circle 16km (10 miles) around, from the waterfront at Shimbashi to Kanda. Streams and inlets were diverted to create three concentric rings of moats and canals, spanned by 30 bridges and defended by 110 gates. The inner moat was faced with stone walls nearly 5m (16ft) thick (some sections are still in place). The huge slabs of granite were brought by barge to Edo from the Izu Peninsula, some 97km (60 miles) away, hauled to the site on sledges, and fitted into place with amazing precision by thousands of stonemasons from all over the country. Most of the Tokugawa-period buildings were destroyed by fire during the 1860s and 1870s, and whole sections of wall were pulled down in the late 19th century as the city expanded. The palace grounds suffered further damage in the World War II firebombings of 1945; only two of the original 28 armouries and three of the original watchtowers survive.

Kaminari-mon Gate at the Asakusa Kannon Temple

Imperial state carriage, East Garden

East Garden

The inner palace grounds are open to the public only on 23 December and 2 January, but visitors can enjoy the outer grounds year-round. Don't miss the **East Garden** ❷ (Tue–Thur, Sat–Sun 9am–4.30pm, Nov–Feb until 4pm; free), entered through Ote-mon Gate; in the Edo period, this was the main gate to the shogun's castle (the present structure is a 1967 restoration). Inside, on the right is the **Museum of the Imperial Collections** ❸, an exhibition hall for art treasures of the Imperial Family. Further along the path, also on the right, is a small rest house where you can buy a map of the grounds.

The path leads uphill. Where it splits are two 19th-century garrison buildings. The larger of the two is the **Hundred-Man Guardhouse** (Hyakunin Bansho); here, the approach to the inner circles of the fortress was defended by four shifts of 100 soldiers each. To the left, the path continues to the *hon-maru* – the innermost part of the castle – where the shogun had his private residence, his audience hall and the *o-oku* (quarters for his wives, concubines and ladies-in-waiting). To the right, the path leads to a formal garden, with a pond, a waterfall and a tea pavilion.

Outer Garden and Nijubashi Bridge

Turn right as you leave the East Garden. Your stroll along the perimeter of the palace grounds will take you past most of the surviving Edo-period buildings: the Fujimi Watchtower, the Fujimi Armoury, the Tatsumi Double-Tiered Watchtower, the Kikyo-mon and Sakashita-mon gates. A few minutes' walk will bring you to the Imperial Palace Outer Garden. This area, where Ieyasu's trusted barons had their villas, was used by the new Meiji government for its first modern ministry buildings. In 1899, when the ministries moved south to Kasumigaseki, it was turned into a public promenade and planted with stands of Japanese pine. At the end of the promenade are **Nijubashi Bridge ❹** and **Sei-mon Gate**. In the background, across the bridge, is the 17th-century Fushimi Watchtower. To the left, as you face the bridge, is **Sakurada-mon** (Gate of the Cherry-Tree Field), the most impressive of the surviving *masu* (box) fortifications that were designed to isolate and pin down intruders.

Nijubashi Bridge

Along the Moat

Continue clockwise around the palace moat. Southwest of the grounds is the granite facade of the **National Diet building ❺** (Kokkai Gijido) where the upper and lower houses of parliament sit. Completed in 1936 after 17 years of work, the building resembles a reconstruction of the Mausoleum of Halicarnassus, one of the seven wonders of the ancient world.

North of here are the Supreme Court and the National Theatre. The 1968 **Supreme Court building**

(Saiko Saibansho) was one of the last projects in the reconstruction of Tokyo after World War II. It is an imposing Modernist composition of stone slabs, long grey walls with narrow slotted windows and cantilevers of steel and concrete.

Iwamoto Hiroyuki's **National Theatre** (Kokuritsu Gekijo) was built in 1966. Drawing on native architectural traditions, it is far more user-friendly than the court building; the building is inspired by the *azekura* (storehouse) style of the 8th-century Shosoin Imperial Repository in Nara. Performances in the two halls of the complex (1,746 and 630 seats respectively) are mainly of kabuki, *bunraku* (puppet theatre) and traditional music and dance.

National Museum of Modern Art

Continue along the moat, passing by the British Embassy compound, until you come to a traffic light at the top of the hill. The cherry trees in this area are particularly lovely in full bloom. Turn right here and you can complete your nearly 5km (3-mile) circuit of the palace grounds. You'll return to the Ote-mon Gate and the East Gardens by way of the **Harakawa-mon Gate**, which has the only surviving wooden bridge over the moat. This gate was originally used by the ladies of the shogun's seraglio on the rare occasions when they were allowed to leave the palace. On the opposite side of the street, at Takebashi, is the **National Museum of Modern Art ❻** (Tue–Sun 10am–5pm, Fri until 8pm; charge, extra for special exhibitions; www.momat.go.jp). The permanent collection includes works by Fujita Tsuguji and Umehara Ryuzaburo, the early masters of 20th-century Western-style art in Japan.

Shrine of Peace

Another way to continue this walk is to go straight north through the traffic light at the top of the hill, away from the palace, to **Yasukuni-jinja ❼** (Shrine of Peace for the Nation;

daily 6am–6pm). This sacred space, dedicated in 1869, honours the souls of those who have died for Japan in battle since 1853, when the armed conflicts began that led to the restoration of the Meiji emperor. Japan's constitution renounces war as an instrument of national policy, and the Japanese are suspicious of anything that smacks of militarism. But this does not prevent many thousands of them from coming here every year to pray for the repose of lost loved ones. The principal buildings are the Main Hall and the Hall of Worship, both in the style of the ancient Grand Shrine at Ise, and the **Yushukan** (Military Museum; 9am–5pm; charge), a museum of war memorabilia. The strangest exhibit in the museum is surely a one-man submarine, designed during World War II to be launched from the deck of a ship. A modern, all-glass addition to the main museum has among its exhibits a Zero carrier fighter plane.

A huge *torii* marks the entrance to Yasukuni-jinja

Martial arts and music stadium, the Budokan

Around the Budokan

From Yasukuni you can return to the palace area by way of the **Tayasu-mon**, one of the largest and finest of the original gates in the north wall of Edo Castle and now the entrance to **Kitanomaru Park**. In the park is the **Nippon Budokan ❽**, built for the 1964 Olympics as a martial arts stadium. The Budokan is the major venue in Tokyo for tournaments and exhibitions of judo, karate and Japanese fencing; on occasion, it also doubles as a hall for rock and pop music concerts. The Beatles played a live concert here in 1966 to an ecstatic audience. At the opposite end of the park, nearest the palace, is the **Crafts Gallery** (Tue–Sun 10am–5pm; charge, extra for special exhibitions), part of the National Museum of Modern Art. Housed in a handsome Meiji-period red-brick building, the gallery has an extensive collection of traditional craftwork in textiles, ceramics, wood, bamboo, lacquer and metal.

CENTRAL TOKYO

In the 17th century, a large expanse of swampy ground between Edo Castle and the bay was filled in and reclaimed on the orders of Tokugawa Ieyasu. Today, that area – comprising the Nihombashi, Marunouchi, Yurakucho and Ginza districts – is what we might call the central city.

Historically, this is the city's geographical centre. When the first bridge was built in Nihombashi in the early 17th century over a tributary of the Sumida River, it was officially designated as the starting point for the five major roads connecting Edo with the rest of the country. That designation still stands: a tall black pole on the bridge, barely noticeable under the expressway overpass, is the 'Zero Kilometre' marker for the national highway system.

Nihombashi and Marunouchi

The city's oldest and weightiest business institutions have their headquarters in **Nihombashi** and **Marunouchi** (and the adjacent Otemachi financial district). Some of Japan's most successful entrepreneurs and corporations have also been avid collectors of art, and it was here that they endowed some of the city's best private museums. These venues have, somewhat ironically, played a key role in the neighbourhoods' attempts to reinvent themselves as cultural and lifestyle destinations in the face of a souring economy.

Bridgestone Museum of Art

Chief among them is the **Bridgestone Museum of Art** ❾ (Tue–Thur, Sat–Sun 10am–6pm, Fri until 8pm; charge; www. bridgestone-museum.gr.jp), on Chuo-dori, between the Kyobashi and Nihombashi stations on the Ginza subway line. This is an eclectic private collection of French Impressionist and School of Paris paintings (Matisse, Renoir, Cézanne,

Modigliani), prints (Rembrandt, Manet, Picasso) and early modern Japanese painting in Western styles. The collection, assembled by Bridgestone Tire Company founder Ishibashi Shojiro, also includes sculptures and artefacts from ancient Egypt and classical Rome and Greece.

Not in the same category at all, but well worth a detour (especially if you are travelling with children) is the charming little **Kite Museum** (Mon–Sat 11am–5pm; charge; tel: 3271-2465), just off Showa-dori and a few minutes' walk from Nihombashi station. Making and flying ornamental kites are old traditions in Japan, and the museum exhibits hand-painted kites in the typical styles of every region of the country. Its 2,000-strong collection also includes kites from around the world.

Idemitsu Museum of Arts

In the opposite direction from the Bridgestone, near Yurakucho station and the southeast corner of the Imperial Palace grounds, is the **Idemitsu Museum of Arts** ❿ (Tue–Sun 10am–5pm, Fri until 7pm; charge; www.idemitsu.com/museum). The Idemitsu has major collections of Chinese

Tokyo Station

The first railway in Japan was built to link Shinbashi with Yokohama. Eventually, the terminus was moved a few kilometres north to the site where the JR Tokyo station stands, directly in front of the Imperial Palace. The handsome red-brick station building on the Marunouchi side, modelled after Amsterdam station, was completed in 1914 and survived the devastating Great Kanto Earthquake of 1923 and the air raids of World War II (though badly damaged each time). While none of the red-brick office buildings that once characterised the Marunouchi district survive – the area is all high-rise towers now – the station has, remarkably, escaped redevelopment and is listed as a City Heritage Site.

JR Tokyo station in Marunouchi

porcelain (Tang and Song dynasties) and Japanese ceramics; the latter includes exceptional examples of the classic Japanese kiln styles – Old Seto, Oribe, Old Kutani, Karatsu and Kakiemon ware. There are also outstanding examples of Zen painting and calligraphy, woodblock prints and genre paintings of the Edo period. Due to the size of the collection, the exhibits are rotated. Archaeology is well represented here, too, in the collection of ancient pottery fragments from all over the world.

Naka-dori

Around the corner from the Idemitsu is the stately Naka-dori, a wide, cobblestoned street bookended by the Peninsula Tokyo Hotel and the Shin-Marunouchi shopping and dining complex. Take a left and walk two blocks, and on your right is the delightful Marunouchi Brick Square. Here you'll find the small but well-appointed **Mitsubishi Ichigokan Museum**

Tokyo International Forum

(Thur–Sat 10am–8pm, Tue–Wed, Sun 10am–6pm; charge; http://mimt.jp/english), which specialises in Japanese and European art from 1880–1890. It also houses about 250 works by Henri de Toulouse-Lautrec.

Tokyo International Forum

A block east of the Idemitsu is the **Tokyo International Forum ⑪**, completed in 1997. Designed by Raphael Vinoly, the Forum is an arrangement of two buildings divided by an open-air promenade. The structure to the east, parallel to the Yamanote line railway tracks, is a breathtaking atrium-style exhibition hall with a 55m (180ft) –high ceiling; the west building is a complex of six halls for conferences, exhibitions and concerts. It's worth a visit to see how one project can utterly transform the shape and feel of an urban space. An excellent, open-air antiques market takes place here on the first and third Sunday of every month.

Just west of the Idemitsu Museum is Hibiya-dori, the broad avenue that runs along the outer gardens of the Imperial Palace. Turn left on this street and you come almost immediately to the **Dai-ichi Mutual Life Insurance Company building** (10am–4pm; tel: 3216-1211). This building survived the bombings of World War II virtually intact and was taken over during the post-war occupation by the Supreme Command of the Allied Powers. General Douglas MacArthur – whom the Japanese dubbed, with a mixture of awe and resentment, 'Emperor' MacArthur – had his office here; the room, which is not open to the public, is kept exactly as it was. Although the core structure remains, the building underwent extensive renovation several years ago.

Hibiya Park and Environs

Walk southwest from the Dai-ichi building on Hibiya-dori, past the intersection of Harumi-dori. Across the avenue on your right is **Hibiyakoen** ⑫, Japan's first Western-style public park, which dates from 1903. Turn left at the Imperial Hotel and one block east, on the corner, you will see the **Takarazuka Theatre**. This all-singing, all-dancing, all-girl revue is a kind of kabuki in reverse, with costumes and sets that would put Busby Berkeley's elaborate Hollywood musicals to shame. The revue was founded in 1913 in Osaka, and the theatre in Tokyo is home to just one of the Takarazuka Revue's five full-time companies, with legions of adoring fans all over the country – mainly teenage girls and middle-aged women.

Yurakucho and Ginza

The name **Yurakucho** means 'Pleasure Quarter' – although this neighbourhood didn't really begin to offer the diversions to be had in Asakusa or Shinjuku until after World War II. In those days it was a red-light district for the occupation troops and (in the area under the railroad tracks) a major black

The San-ai Building, a Tokyo icon at Ginza 4-chome intersection

market. Later, the area became famous for its rows of cheap *yakitori* and noodle restaurants, most of them open to the elements, where office workers from Ginza would gather at night for beer and conversation.

In the Edo period, Sukiyabashi was the name of a bridge from the villa of one of the shogun's trusted vassals (a noted tea master) over a moat to a silver mint that Ieyasu established here in 1612. The silver mint (in Japanese, *ginza*) gave the area its name, and it stuck. In 1872 a fire destroyed much of Ginza, and the new Meiji government ordered it rebuilt in Western style, with a grid of streets and avenues, pavements and streetlights, and horse-drawn streetcars. In the same year, the country's first railway line went into service, running from nearby Shimbashi to Yokohama – and **Ginza** became chic.

More particularly, it became *the* place for shopping. Here rose the great emporia – founded in the Edo period – that would transform themselves into modern palaces of consumerism: Mitsukoshi, Matsuzakaya, Takashimaya and Matsuya. The landmark Hattori clock tower went up in 1932 on the facade of what is now the fashionable Wako department store, on the Ginza 4-chome intersection. Virtually next door is the flagship Mikimoto store, the first shop in Tokyo to sell the famous cultured pearls. The newer Ginza Mikimoto 2 is an eye-catching pink tower with irregular, cellular-shaped windows and a very chic restaurant and wine cellar. Back towards Yurakucho station is the Sony showroom, where you can test-run the latest high-tech electronics equipment.

The area has lost little of its cachet: new luxury stores continue to open, many with eye-popping contemporary facades (check out the Hermès building and Chanel's spectacular LED-screen frontage). Those with the wherewithal can spend considerable time and money here. But even casual visitors with limited budgets will revel in the window-shopping and people-watching opportunities. The best time to visit is at dusk, as the lights start to come on, illuminating the shops; or join the strollers on Sunday afternoons, when Chuo-dori (the main north–south avenue) is closed to traffic.

Kabuki-za

For something completely different from these glitzy shopfronts, head south along Harumi-dori. You'll soon come across the red lanterns, long banners and posters of the **Kabuki-za** ⑬ (see page 84) on your left. The first kabuki theatre was built on this site in 1889. The Kabuki-za building of 1925 was designed to invoke the

Streets of Ginza

castle architecture of the Tokugawa period; it was destroyed in an air raid in 1945 and rebuilt in 1951, then again in 2011.

SHITAMACHI

A vast expanse of seven city wards, Shitamachi lies in the eastern and northern parts of Tokyo. Its districts are traditional neighbourhoods where you will find rows of one- and two-storey houses, small factories and shops. You'll also find a number of temples, shrines and museums, plus some of the largest shopping areas.

Asakusa

This district is the spiritual heart of Shitamachi and the working-class traditions that gave birth to the culture of the Edo period. The focal point and main attraction is **Senso-ji**, better known as the **Asakusa Kannon Temple** (daily Apr–Sept 6am–5pm, Oct–Mar 6.30am–5pm; tel: 3842-0181). According to legend, the temple houses a small statue of the Buddhist goddess of mercy that was found in the Sumida River by two fishermen from the village of Asakusa, on the outskirts of Edo, in the year 628. In fact, not even the temple priests have ever seen the statue, and there is no real evidence that it exists. For nearly 1,000 years it was merely an object of local veneration.

However, when Edo became the capital of the Tokugawa shogunate, the village acquired importance as an entertainment quarter. That was especially so in the early 19th century, when for a brief period the kabuki theatres were located here. The Meiji restoration and the opening of Japan to new Western-style amusements only enhanced Asakusa's reputation as 'Fun City': the country's first photography studios appeared here in 1875; the first place in Japan to call itself a 'bar' opened in Asakusa in 1880 (and is still doing business); the first cinema opened in 1903. Before long, the streets and alleys of Asakusa

Kaminari-mon, the main entrance to Senso-ji

were filled with music halls, burlesque theatres, cabarets, gambling dens and watering holes of every description.

Most of the temple quarter was firebombed to ashes in 1945, but by 1958 the people of the area had raised enough money to rebuild Senso-ji and all of the important structures around it. So what if the restorations are in concrete rather than the original wood? The temple area is not merely a tourist attraction but a complex discourse on the possibilities of urban life.

Kaminari-mon Gate and Nakamise-dori

Start your exploration from Asakusa station, on the Ginza subway line (Tokyo's first subway, from Asakusa to Ueno, began here in 1927). A few steps from the station exit is **Kaminari-mon** ⑭ (Thunder Gate), the main entrance to Senso-ji, hung with a pair of enormous red paper lanterns. The two figures in the alcoves of the gate are the guardian gods of the temple, placed there to ward off evil spirits: the Thunder God (Kaminari no Kami) on the left, the Wind God (Kaze no Kami) on the right.

From Kaminari-mon, a long, narrow arcade called **Nakamise-dori** – crowded wall to wall with visitors – leads to the temple grounds. Shops along the arcade sell toasted rice crackers, pepper spices in gourd-shaped wooden bottles, dolls and toys, fans, children's kimono ornaments and souvenirs of all sorts. Some of these shops have been operated by the same families for hundreds of years.

The arcade ends at a two-storey gate called the **Hozo-mon** ⓯ (Treasury Gate). The huge straw sandals on the back wall of the gate are for the benefit of its guardian gods, should either of them want to leave his alcove and take a stroll. Off to the left is the temple administration building, where you can get free

Touring in Style

An alternative way to get to Senso-ji is to take the glassed-in, double-decker rice ferry that departs regularly throughout the day from Hi-node Pier or from Hama Rikyu (Detached Palace Garden) for the 35-minute ride upriver to Asakusa. The Sumida River was once a vital artery, especially for the timber yards of nearby Kiba. The ferry service dates back to 1885, and some people still use it to commute to work, although most passengers now are tourists. It is by no stretch of the imagination a scenic cruise, but the glimpses of Tokyo's post-industrial underside provide a fascinating alternative view of the city.

Once you reach Asakusa and have visited Senso-ji, you can rest your weary feet by chartering a rickshaw. The comfy, well-sprung, two-person carriages are pulled around the tourist sites by young men dressed in traditional work clothes. They're not cheap, though: count on paying around ¥10,000 for two people for an hour. Look for them outside the Kaminari-mon Gate.

tickets to visit the garden of
the abbot's residence, called
the Denbo-in (see page 45).

Main Hall and the Asakusa Shrine

Directly across the courtyard from the Hozo-mon is
the main hall of Senso-ji; to
the left is the **Five-Storey
Pagoda**. On the way to the
main hall, it is customary
to stop at the huge bronze

Souvenir stalls line Nakamise-dori

incense burner to bathe one's hands and face in the smoke (an
observance believed to bestow a year's worth of good health
on the worshipper), or to direct the smoke to any part of the
body that is ailing.

The building to the right as you face the main hall is the
Asakusa-jinja, also known as Sanja Sanma. Built in 1649 and
one of the few buildings in the area to survive the bombing
raids of 1945, this is a Shinto shrine dedicated to the legendary founders of Senso-ji. A purge on the Buddhist clergy during the Meiji period separated Buddhist temples and Shinto
shrines, but in these more harmonious days it is not uncommon to find the two faiths sharing the same grounds. The
Sanja Matsuri, held here every year on the third weekend in
May, is the biggest, most exuberant festival in Tokyo.

Around Bentenyama

Walk back from Asakusa-jinja in the direction of the Kaminari-
mon Gate along the narrow street to the left of the Nakamise-
dori arcade. You will first come to **Bentenyama**, a little hill
with a shrine to the Goddess of Good Fortune, and to a 17th-
century belfry called **Toki-no-kane**. In the Edo period, the

Senso-ji's main hall

bell was used to toll the hours for the people of Asakusa; it still rings every morning, when the temple grounds open.

Take time to browse in the row of shops opposite Bentenyama. Nakaya sells festival costumes and regalia for the annual Sanja Matsuri. Hyakusuke specialises in handmade brushes, cosmetics and theatrical make-up for kabuki actors, geisha and traditional weddings. It's the only shop left in Tokyo that still sells skin cleanser made from powdered nightingale droppings (ladies of the Edo period used it religiously). Fujiya sells stencil-dyed cotton hand towels called *tenugui* in hundreds of different traditional Edo-period motifs.

Turn at the corner, cross the arcade, and you come to still more fascinating small shops and ateliers. Yonoya, for example (on the left side of the street), sells handmade boxwood combs in the special shapes and sizes required for traditional Japanese coiffures and wigs; the family business dates back about 300 years.

Denbo-in

Further along this street, on the right, is the wooden gate to **Denbo-in** (daily 9am–4pm; free with pass obtained at temple administration building), the abbot's garden. The garden, with its intricate design of ponds, trees and flowering shrubs, is thought to have been created by the tea master, architect and poet Kobori Enshu (1579–1647). Very few people seem to know how to get in – most of the time, the garden is empty.

Kappabashi

Turn south, away from Denbo-in on any side street, and return to Asakusa-dori, the broad avenue where you first found Kaminari-mon. Turn right, walk to the end of the avenue and cross Kokusai-dori. Located two blocks west is **Kappabashi**, Tokyo's wholesale restaurant-supply district. The people who do business here never imagined the area would become a tourist attraction, but it has, and with good reason. What Japanese customers see as merely the tools of their trade, foreign visitors have discovered as low-cost, imaginative gifts to take home.

Stop at Maizuru, for example, for plastic food – the realistic-looking plastic food replicas you see in display windows in Japan's neighbourhood restaurants, noodle shops and sushi bars. Nishimura, across the street, specialises in the decorated divided curtains called *noren*, usually made of cotton or linen, that hang in the doorways of shops; they make wonderful wall displays and room dividers. Kondo Shoten, in the next block, sells a huge variety of bamboo trays, baskets, scoops

Five-Storey Pagoda

Kitchenware in Kappabashi

and containers. Nearby Iida Shoten is the place to look for hand-figured cast-iron kettles and casserole dishes, a craft tradition of the Tohoku region in the far northeast of Japan. On the narrow side street that leads back to Kokusai-dori, on the left, is Tsubaya Hochoten, *the* place for professional kitchen cutlery – especially the long, hand-forged, steel knives used by sushi chefs. Most shops in Kappabashi are open daily 9am to 6pm.

Along Kokusai-dori, in the first block north of the Asakusa-dori intersection, you will see several shops selling Buddhist altars (or *butsudan*) that enshrine the spirits of one's ancestors. No Japanese household would be without one; the most expensive *butsudan*, hand-carved in precious woods and covered with gold leaf, can cost millions of yen.

Tokyo Skytree
Looming above Asakusa from just across the Sumida River, the 634m (2,080ft) **Tokyo Skytree** ⑯ debuted in 2012 as the

world's tallest tower (and, after the 830m/2,723ft Burj Khalifa in Dubai, the second tallest structure of any kind in the world). The tower's official function is to serve as a broadcast facility for TV and radio networks, but Skytree is also the centrepiece of a complex that includes offices, shops, restaurants and an aquarium. Two observation decks are open to the public at 350m (1,150ft) and 450m (1,476ft); reservations for visiting them can be made online (www.tokyo-skytree.jp).

Ryogoku Kokugikan

Serving as the venue for three of the six major sumo tournaments each year, **Ryogoku Kokugikan** ⑰ is the home of Japan's official sport. The 13,000-seat stadium stands more than 60m (196ft) tall and is capped by a copper-plated roof meant to resemble a traditional storehouse. There is also a museum devoted to sumo history (daily 10am–4.30pm; free; www.sumo.or.jp), so it's worth a visit even if no tournament is taking place. The neighbourhood around the stadium is home to many *sumo-beya* (training stables), making encounters with

Exploring Shitamachi

If you have visited Asakusa and have time to explore more of Shitamachi, the area just to the north of Ueno Park is worth a half-day or even more. The districts of Yanaka, Nezu and Sendagi form a quiet, low-rise, low-stress reminder of what life in the city used to be like. There are winding alleys, sudden steep flights of stairs, ancient temples and numerous old wooden houses, shops and restaurants.

Yanaka Cemetery is a popular place for viewing (and partying under) the cherry blossoms. From Nippori station (on the JR Yamanote line) take the stairs up the hillside to the cemetery. After wandering through Yanaka, make your way down to Nezu and explore the handsome Shinto shrine. Then finish the day with dinner at Hantei (see page 108).

Tokyo Skytree

the man-mountains more than likely.

Ueno

The newly refurbished JR station at **Ueno** was for decades the end of the line from the underdeveloped provinces of the northeast. In the Edo period, however, the hill behind the station was a seat of great power. In 1625 the shogun Hidetaka, Ieyasu's son, established a temple here called Kan'ei-ji to protect the capital from evil spirits. By the end of the 17th century, its various halls, shrines and subtemples were spread all over the hill.

Kan'ei-ji's glory and influence were tied entirely to the Tokugawa dynasty, and it suffered the same fate. In 1868, when the shogunate surrendered to the armies of the imperial party, a small force of some 2,000 Tokugawa retainers – young hotheads for the most part – refused to accept the transfer of power and occupied the hill. They might have had righteous convictions, but the other side had all the cannon. The imperial forces surrounded the hill and attacked, with predictable results. A few rebels fled; those who remained set fire to Kan'ei-ji and committed ritual suicide.

The new government turned the hill into the 53-hectare (131-acre) public **Ueno Park ⑱**. They restored whatever had survived of the temple complex, adding those improvements that the much-admired Western world defined as modern and cosmopolitan: museums, concert halls, a library, a university of fine arts, a zoo. The Ueno district might not be the first stop on any visitor's itinerary, but it will well reward whatever time you can make for it, especially if you happen to be visiting in the middle of April, when the cherry blossom in the park is glorious.

Museum of Western Art

Directly across the street from the park exit at Ueno station (on the JR Yamanote line) is the **Tokyo Metropolitan Festival Hall**. Built in 1961, it is one of the city's major venues for classical music. There's no particular reason to explore it – the architecture is undistinguished – but don't miss the **National Museum of Western Art** (Tue–Sun 9.30am–5.30pm, Fri until 8pm; charge, extra charge for special exhibitions; www.nmwa.go.jp), opposite the Festival Hall on the right. The museum has some 850 French Impressionist paintings, prints and drawings – including works by Renoir, Monet and Cézanne – that were originally the private collection of a rich businessman named Kojiro Matsukata, who left it to the nation in his will. The museum's rather eclectic acquisitions also feature paintings by Rubens, El Greco and Jackson Pollock. The building itself was designed by Le Corbusier. The Rodin sculptures in the courtyard – *Gates of Hell*, *Thinker* and the magnificent *Burghers of Calais* – are authentic castings from the sculptor's original moulds.

Ueno Park

Tokyo National Museum

Tokyo National Museum

Walk northeast from the National Museum of Western Art, past the National Museum of Science, turn left on the avenue that bisects the park, and you come to the four buildings of the **Tokyo National Museum** ⓲ (Hyokeikan, Honkan, Toyokan and Horyu-ji Treasure Hall; Tue–Sun 9.30am–5pm, Apr–Sept Sat–Sun until 6pm; charge, extra for special exhibitions; www.tnm.go.jp/en). If you make one stop in Ueno, this should be it: the TNM has one of the world's best collections of East Asian art and prehistory.

The oldest part of the complex, the Hyokeikan, dates back to 1909. It has only nine exhibition rooms, but the displays of Jomon-period pottery (*c*.3500BC–2000BC), and 4th- to 7th-century terracotta tomb figures called *haniwa*, are fascinating. The two-storey Horyu-ji Treasure Hall houses some 320 wooden sculptures, scrolls, and other works of art, originally the property of the 7th-century Horyu-ji Temple in Nara. The exhibits in the main building, the Honkan, are of Japanese paintings, calligraphy, sculpture, textiles, ceramics, swords and armour. The Toyokan, the most recent addition to the complex (1968), is devoted to the art of other Asian cultures. Altogether, the museum has some 90,000 objects in its permanent collection or on loan from shrines and temples – among them are 84 works that are designated by the government as National Treasures.

Behind the museum, to the northwest, is the *hondo* (main hall) of **Kan'ei-ji**, rebuilt in 1879 after a fire and looking a bit the worse for wear. Perhaps its most impressive feature is the ornamental gate that originally led to the mausoleum of the fifth shogun, Tsunayoshi.

Ueno Zoo

Walk south from Kan'ei-ji on the road that circles the park, following the signs for **Ueno Zoo** (Tue–Sun 9.30am–5pm; charge). Opened in 1882, the zoo now comprises two areas, 14 hectares (35 acres) in total, connected by a bridge and a monorail. The zoo is 'home' to some 900 species, although by present-day standards most of the habitats are primitive and uncomfortable. What draws most of the Japanese visitors here is the family of giant pandas, housed near the main entrance. If they don't seem to belong here, neither does the five-storey Kan'ei-ji Pagoda, which somehow wound up on the grounds of the zoo in the process of expansion.

Tosho-gu Shrine

Just to the east of the zoo is **Tosho-gu ⑳**, the shrine to the first Tokugawa shogun, Ieyasu, who died in 1616. The Imperial Court declared him a god, and a great sanctum was consecrated to his spirit at Nikko, in the mountains of the present-day Nagano Prefecture. That was the original and foremost Tosho-gu. The one here in Ueno was built a few years later, in the same Chinese-inspired style, with almost every available

Penguins at Ueno Zoo

surface carved and painted in elaborate natural and geometrical motifs. The entrance to the shrine is marked by a stone arch and a path lined with some 200 stone lanterns; the lantern just inside the grounds is some 5.5m (over 18ft) high – one of the three largest in Japan. Tosho-gu has survived the fires of 1868, the Great Kanto Earthquake of 1923 and the bombings of 1945. That makes it one of the few authentic Edo-period buildings left in Tokyo. The shrine itself, its magnificent Chinese gate and most of the works of art it houses, are registered as National Treasures.

From Tosho-gu, follow the signs to the *koban* (police substation), more or less in the middle of the park, and turn south on the avenue that leads to the main entrance. Off to the right is the **Saiyoken**, one of many Shinto shrines in Japan dedicated to Sugawara no Michizane, a Heian nobleman of the 9th century. A distinguished court poet, Michizane was falsely accused of plotting against the emperor and died in exile, but later came to be worshipped as Tenjin, the patron spirit of scholarship. In February and March, students all over the country pay homage at his various shrines to pray for success in their entrance exams.

Kiyomizu Kannon Hall

Just south of the shrine is the Kuro-mon, a gate which leads to the **Kiyomizu Kannon** hall. Part of the original Kan'ei-ji complex, Kiyomizu was built on the model of the larger and more famous Kiyomizu Temple in Kyoto. The deities worshipped here are the Senju Kannon (the Goddess of Mercy) and the Kosodate Kannon, invoked for help with problems of infertility and difficult childbirth. Registered as a National Treasure, this is another of the few buildings that survived the battle of 1868.

A City of Flowers

Whatever the season, there are always blossoms visible in Tokyo – not just in the parks but even the narrowest backstreets. Camellia (*tsubaki*), Japanese apricot (*ume*) and quince (*karin*) bring colour to drab late winter. Spring arrives with a rush in late March, with spectacular arrays of various cherries (*sakura*), the most glorious of which are the *somei-yoshino*, as their profuse, pure-white blossoms open before any leaves emerge. After the azaleas (*tsutsuji*) and trellises of purple wisteria (*fuji*) are over, the rainy season brings irises (*shobu/ayame*), gardenias (*kuchinashi*) and hydrangeas (*ajisai*). In midsummer, look for lotus flowers (*hasu*) in temple ponds and morning glories (*asagao*) trained up the front of houses. Once the autumn displays of chrysanthemums (*kiku*) are over, it's the turning leaves that catch the eye, especially the scarlet maples (*momiji*) and bright-yellow ginkgo (*itcho*). And even when there is snow on the ground, you may see peonies (*botan*) carefully protected under little eaves.

Statue of Takamori Saigo

Further south, the park narrows to a point, with two flights of steps leading down to the main entrance. At the top of the steps is the **statue of Takamori Saigo**, commander of the imperial army that overthrew the shogunate in 1868 and, briefly, the head of the Meiji government. Saigo is a problematic hero in Japanese history; by 1871 he had fallen out with the other Meiji leaders and was killed in an unsuccessful rebellion.

From the park entrance turn right and walk west. A few minutes' walk brings you to the grounds of Shinobazu Pond.

Shitamachi Museum

Just inside the entrance to the grounds, on the right, is the **Shitamachi Museum** ㉑ (Tue–Sun 9.30am–4.30pm; charge; tel: 3823-7451). Budget some time for this museum: it will give you a wonderfully concrete sense of the lifestyle that defined this part of the city for well over 300 years. The displays on the first floor include reproductions of a *nagaya* (one of the long, single-storey terrace houses once strung together in the maze of narrow streets of the city's downtown districts), with an atelier and a merchant's shop; visitors are welcome to take off their shoes and walk on the woven mats in the *tatami* rooms. On the second floor are displays of tools and furnishings. There is a video library on traditional

Shitamachi crafts, a good booklet in English and occasional hands-on demonstrations.

Shinobazu Pond

If you've planned a full day for Ueno, you should still have enough of it left for a walk along the path from the museum around **Shinobazu Pond**. The pond was reclaimed from Tokyo Bay in the 17th century, and was redesigned by Tenkai, the first abbot of Kan'ei-ji. In the middle of the island he created **Benten-do**, a shrine to Benten, one of the Seven Gods of Good Luck; patron goddess of the arts, she is usually depicted holding a lute. The shrine was destroyed in 1945 and rebuilt on the original model. The pond has three sections. The north is part of Ueno Zoo, the western section has rowing boats and swan-shaped pedalos for hire and the larger southern section, containing a bird sanctuary, is famous for its great pink lotuses, which blossom in July and August.

Ameyoko Market

From the Shitamachi Museum, it's a short walk north on Chuo-dori to the main entrance of the Ueno railway station. Across the road is **Ameya Yokocho** market (more familiarly, Ameyoko), a warren of side streets and alleys with hundreds of small shops and stalls stretching south to the Okachimachi stop on the Hibiya subway line. Just after World War II this was a black-market quarter for the precious supplies of food that farmers would bring in from the northeast. Today the

Ameyoko market

trade here centres on copies of designer bags and accessories, watches and jewellery – and, once again, food. Ameyoko is the best place in Tokyo to buy the delicacies served in traditional New Year meals. During the last days of December, as many as half a million people come here to stock up for the holiday.

Akihabara

No neighbourhood has done more to boost Tokyo's cachet in recent years than **Akihabara**, which has morphed from a retail electronics district to the capital of Japan Cool. Go out of the 'Electric Town' exit of JR Akihabara station, cross the main Chuo-dori strip, and you'll find alleys full of shops catering to fans of animated films, manga comics, video games and plastic figurines, with spin-off businesses like maid cafés, costume shops and event halls. Akihabara has retained its seedier elements – the AV ('adult video') industry has a strong presence here – but the legions of enthusiastic *otaku* (fanboys) lend the streets a festive air. All the retail electronics giants operate at least one store in the area, with a massive branch of the Yodobashi Camera chain having joined the ranks of LAOX, Yamagiwa and Sofmap. Most of the larger stores have floors with goods for export, at duty-free prices (you'll need to show your passport). Loop back towards the station and explore the Tokyo Anime Center (www.animecenter.jp), a gallery, retail and event space in the huge UDX Building.

Electronics shop in Akihabara

Kanda Myojin Shrine

Shopping need not be your only motive for a visit to

this area. From Akihabara station, head north on Chuo-dori to the next major intersection. Turn left onto Kuramaebashi-dori (at Suehirocho station on the Ginza line) and after five minutes a flight of steps on your left leads up to the **Kanda Myojin Shrine** ㉒.

Kanda Myojin is dedicated to three deities. Okuninushi no Mikoto and Sukunahikona no Mikoto are gods that figure in Japanese creation myths, while Taira no Masakado, a Heian nobleman executed for treason in 940, became a revered figure and worshipped spirit. Masakado

Kanda Myojin Shrine

led the first revolt by the emerging warrior class against the Imperial Court in Kyoto, and tried to establish an independent state in eastern Japan (with himself as its emperor). The people of Kanda – themselves no great respecters of remote authority – pray to the spirit of Masakado when they have struggles of their own to face.

The shrine was relocated here in 1616 from the area which has become the Otemachi financial district; the original wooden buildings were destroyed in the earthquake of 1923 and rebuilt in concrete. Some of the smaller buildings on the grounds of the shrine contain the *mikoshi* (portable shrines) that are carried through the streets of this quarter in one of Tokyo's three major celebrations, the Kanda Matsuri.

From the main (south) gate of the shrine to the *torii* arch at the foot of the hill, the street is lined with shops selling the special delicacies of this neighbourhood: *miso* (fermented bean paste) and sweet rice drinks flavoured with ground ginger. Across the avenue from the arch are the grounds of **Yushima Seido** ❷❸, founded in 1632 in Ueno as an academy for the study of Confucian classics and moved here in 1691. The academy was established to train the Tokugawa government's ruling elite in the virtues of hierarchy, obedience and self-control; it is now a shrine. A statue of Confucius presides over the path to the sombre, all-black main hall, which has burned down six times in its long history. The current temple, with its wide, stone-flagged courtyard, dates from 1935.

Turn right as you leave the shrine, and you soon come to Hijiri-bashi, the bridge over the Kanda River at Ochanomizu station on the JR crosstown Sobu line. Just south of the station is **Nikolai Cathedral** ❷❹, the centre of the Russian Orthodox Church in Japan. Officially, this church is called the Holy Resurrection Cathedral. But it is better known by the name of its founder, St Nikolai Kassatkin (1836–1912), a Russian who came to Japan in 1861 and spent the rest of his life here as an Orthodox missionary. A short walk downhill along Meiji-dori takes you to the fascinating bookshop district of **Jimbocho**. Sanseido has new books in English, while Kitazawa and Isseido stock second-hand and antiquarian titles, but the best finds can be found at the ramshackle shops jamming the area's side streets.

YAMANOTE (WESTERN TOKYO)

We now head uptown to the western Yamanote districts. Tokyo gets younger and hipper as you move west; it also gets greener and less claustrophobic. Yamanote has the lion's share of the city's fashionable stores and Western-style restaurants. It also has most of the parks, gardens and open spaces. There's less cultural history here, but you will have much more opportunity to sit back and contemplate it than you will ever have in Shitamachi.

Akasaka

At one time, this part of the city was notable only for its proximity to the National Diet building and its satellite political office buildings. **Akasaka** was a district of traditional restaurants called *ryotei* (see page 101), where the politicians of the ruling Liberal Democratic

Cherry blossom in Yoyogi Park

Party and their connections in the business world could meet to wheel and deal. A few of the *ryotei* are still operating, but nightlife in Akasaka today caters to a different, younger crowd. By day, however, it has few sights for visitors; you would probably put it on your itinerary only if you had plenty of time to spare.

Hie-jinja shrine ㉕ is one of Akasaka's worthwhile attractions. This shrine was founded in the late 15th century and was under the protection of the Tokugawa shogun. Today it sponsors one of the three largest festivals in Tokyo, the Sanno Matsuri, held in even-numbered years from 9 June to 16 June. The festival features a procession of palanquins and attendants in Edo-period costume. But you can see ceremonies performed at Hie-jinja throughout the year – to safeguard petitioners from traffic accidents. Walk through and you might see a Shinto priest in a white robe blessing a car.

A few minutes further west on Aoyama-dori, on the left, is the **Sogetsu Kaikan**, headquarters of the school of *ikebana* (flower-arranging) founded by Teshigahara Sofu in 1927. In addition to the exhibits, you can view the stone garden in the lobby, which was created by the late Isamu Noguchi, one of the masters of modern sculpture.

Roppongi

Long known as an entertainment district for expats with plenty of discos, clubs, bars and all-night restaurants, Roppongi's lacklustre daytime face has undergone a makeover as the area reinvented itself as an art and lifestyle town. This began in 2003

National Art Center

with the completion of **Roppongi Hills** 26, a complex of shops, restaurants and bars. The **Mori Art Museum** (Wed–Mon 10am–10pm, Tue 10am–5pm; charge; www.mori.art.museum), at the top of the 54-floor Mori Tower, is one of Tokyo's most innovative and daring galleries. The ticket includes admission to the spectacular observation gallery.

An even newer complex, the Midtown Tokyo, houses a similar mix of shops, bars and eateries, plus Midtown Tower. The redesigned **Suntory Art Museum** (Sun–Mon, Wed–Thur 10am–6pm, Fri–Sat 10am–8pm; charge; www.tokyo-midtown.com) has relocated here. Rounding out Roppongi's 'Art Triangle' is the **National Art Center** (Wed–Mon 10am–6pm, Fri until 8pm; charge; www.nact.jp), a highly original design from the late Kisho Kurokawa. The centre has no permanent exhibition, but stages great shows by Japanese and overseas artists.

The sophisticated restaurants and nightclubs of **Nishi-Azabu** and **Hiroo** are to the west of Roppongi, with the silhouette of the 1958 **Tokyo Tower**, a communications mast with an observation deck, to the east.

Aoyama

This neighbourhood at the east end of Omotesando station, across Aoyama-dori, is **Aoyama**, a designer-label territory thick with the boutiques of Issey Miyake, Calvin Klein, Gianfranco Ferre, Missoni and Comme des Garçons, not to mention the remarkable Chanel building, and Aoyama Prada and La Collezione which are architectural landmarks in their own right. Keep your plastic in your pocket for now and press on: at the end of the street, to the right, is another fine-art museum.

The recently renovated **Nezu Institute of Fine Arts** 27 (Tue–Sun 10am–5pm; charge www.nezu-muse.or.jp) houses the private art collection of Meiji-period railroad magnate and

The Dior building in Aoyama

politician Nezu Kaichiro. The institute boasts outstanding works of Japanese painting, calligraphy and ceramics, as well as a collection of ancient Chinese bronze utensils and sculpture. For many visitors, the lasting impression of the institute is its wonderful garden: a composition of pines and flowering shrubs, ponds and waterfalls, moss-covered stone lanterns and tea pavilions laid out on what is still some of the most expensive land in the world.

National Stadium

Back on Aoyama-dori, a brisk 15-minute walk east will bring you to the Meiji-jingu's outer gardens, which embrace **Jingu Stadium** ❷❽ (home field of the Yakult Swallows baseball team), the Prince Chichibu Memorial Rugby Football Ground and the 75,000-seat **National Stadium** – the main venue of the 1964 Summer Olympic Games. Follow Aoyama-dori west instead, and you come eventually to Shibuya, by way of the Aoyama Gakuin University campus on the left, and the United Nations University and the **National Children's Castle** (a huge indoor play area) on the right.

Shibuya

Shibuya is Tokyo's most happening pleasure zone. This is where contemporary clubbing intersects with tween fashion, designer department stores collide with love hotels and snob culture rubs shoulders with sleaze. Thanks to its position as a major transport hub (three subways, three private railways and four JR lines), it is first and foremost a commercial subcentre. While Shibuya boasts department stores, theatres and concert halls, it also has a much earthier aspect, with alleys of cheap bars, restaurants and clubs of all descriptions.

The main intersection by the Hachiko statue (see box, page 64) offers one of the classic views of contemporary Tokyo, with huge video screens and neon. Take a while to observe the carnival of shoppers, buskers, hustlers and hawkers that fills the plaza day and (especially) night. Diagonally across the intersection is the entrance to the Center-gai pedestrian shopping street, with its raucous games arcades, fast-food joints and pubs.

There is little sightseeing here, but if you walk past the Seibu department store and turn up Koen-dori avenue, you will reach the **Tobacco and Salt Museum** ㉙ (Tue–Sun 10am–6pm; charge; www.jti.co.jp/culture/museum), a collection of artefacts associated with tobacco and salt since the days of the Mayan civilisation. Tobacco and salt were both government monopolies until the 1980s, and the Japan Tobacco and Salt Public Corporation made tidy sums from its control of these two substances. The museum was conceived

Urban sprawl

Tokyo's space-starved downtown area has impelled building developers to combine, in a single setting, everything from shopping malls and restaurants to offices, cinemas, museums, apartments, concert halls and hotels. The Tokyo Midtown and Roppongi Hills complexes are the most prominent of these venues; others include Hikarie in Shibuya; Sunshine City in Ikebukuro; Sacas in Akasaka; Tokyo Skytree Town in Shitamachi; and the Marunouchi and Shin-Marunouchi buildings near Tokyo station.

simply as a way to spend some of it. What makes it worth a visit are the exhibitions on the fourth floor, including Edo-period woodblock prints on the themes of smoking and traditional salt production.

At the top of Koen-dori, to the left, is the NHK public television network complex, consisting of the **NHK Broadcasting Centre** and the 4,000-seat NHK Hall auditorium, a major venue in Tokyo for classical music concerts. At the Broadcasting Centre you can take a 'Studio Park' guided tour of NHK's high-tech facilities and programme production; unfortunately, the tours are all in Japanese.

With time to spare, you might stop at **Bunkamura** (Culture Village; www.bunkamura.co.jp) on your way back to Shibuya station. This six-storey complex of theatres and galleries, built by the Tokyu department store, is host to the Tokyo Philharmonic Orchestra, international film festivals and visiting opera and ballet companies. It's an example of how Japan's retail conglomerates invest in culture to create an image for

Man's Best Friend

The statue of Hachiko (at the north plaza entrance to Shibuya station) pays homage to the hero of Japan's best-known 'faithful dog' story. Hachiko's master, a professor at the University of Tokyo, would take the dog with him every morning to this station on his way to school, and Hachiko would go back to the station every evening to meet him on his return. One day in 1925 the professor failed to appear; he had suffered a stroke that day at the university and died. But every evening for the next seven years the dog would go to Shibuya and wait for his master in vain. The story so appealed to the Japanese people that they raised money to buy a statue of Hachiko even before the dog's own death in 1935. The brass statue now in the plaza (a replica) is the rendezvous point for anybody planning to meet a friend in Shibuya.

Pedestrians surge across the Shibuya intersection

themselves. A museum on the lower-level Garden Floor often has exhibits on loan from major European museums.

Harajuku

The area west and south of the JR Harajuku station, between the Meiji shrine and Meiji-dori, is **Harajuku**. Begin your exploration of this area at **Meiji-jingu** ③ (grounds: daily dawn–sunset; free; Imperial Treasure House: Sat–Sun 9am–4pm; charge, separate charge for the Iris Garden in June). The entrance, marked by two huge *torii* gates (the pillars are 1,700-year-old cypress trees), is just a few steps from the Omotesando exit of Harajuku station. This shrine is dedicated to the spirits of Emperor Meiji, who died in 1912, and Empress Shoken. The main buildings on the grounds are the *honden* (sanctum) – destroyed in the air raids of 1945 and restored in 1958 – and the Imperial Treasure House of personal belongings of the emperor and empress. The

Offerings of casks of sake at Meiji-jingu

deification of Emperor Meiji was inevitable; it was he, after all, who presided over the emergence of Japan as a modern nation state. His shrine is surely the most solemn and decorous place in Tokyo. During the annual festival (31 October–3 November) and on New Year's Day, as many as a million people will come here to offer prayers and pay their respects. On Coming-of-Age Day (the 2nd Monday of January) it is a popular venue for young people who have turned 20, with many of the women dressed in gorgeous kimonos. In spring and summer you can admire the irises and flowering shrubs of the inner gardens.

Yoyogi Park

Adjacent to the shrine is **Yoyogi Park**, remarkable chiefly for the **National Yoyogi Sports Centre**: two buildings designed for the 1964 Olympic Games. The larger of the two is the swimming stadium; the smaller is a basketball gym. The park itself was once a parade ground for the Imperial Japanese Army, and after World War II it was taken over by the occupation for military housing, then redeveloped as the Olympic Village site for the Tokyo Games. The infrastructure for the Games, with broad avenues and new subway stops, did wonders for the Harajuku and Omotesando quarter. Suddenly it was accessible, and with access came commerce. By the 1980s, this was perhaps the busiest and trendiest (and demographically youngest) area in Tokyo. Although the rock bands and Elvis impersonators have now been banned, Yoyogi Park is still massively popular with joggers, skateboarders, student groups and face-painted youths spilling out of concerts in the Sports Centre or seeking respite after the crowds and intensity of Takeshita-dori (see page 68).

Sword Museum

North of the park is the **Japanese Sword Museum** (Token Hakubutsukan; Tue–Sun 10am–4.30pm; charge; tel: 3379-1386), a collection of the works of noted swordsmiths. The Japanese have been crafting the finest steel blades since the 8th century. The technique of making and refining carbon steel from iron sand is called *tamahagane*.

Yoyogi Park

Blocks of steel were folded and cross-folded at high temperatures until it had thousands of 'layers', giving extraordinary strength. The block was then hammered into shape and folded around a core of softer steel, making it as flexible as it was strong. Swords were treasured by the warrior caste, as weapons, symbols of spiritual purity and works of art.

Woodblock print by Utamaro

Ukiyo-e Ota Museum of Art

Southeast of the park, on a narrow street just off Omotesando, is the **Ukiyo-e Ota Memorial Museum of Art** ㉛ (Tue–Sun 10.30am–5.30pm; closed last four days of most months; charge; www.ukiyoe-ota-muse.jp). It displays one of Tokyo's finest private collections of traditional woodblock prints called *ukiyo-e*. Here there are some 12,000 prints, including rare works by Hiroshige, Sharaku and Utamaro. The collection is rotated each month.

Takeshita-dori and Togo Shrine

At the bottom of the hill, where Omotesando intersects with Meiji-dori, make a brief detour. Turn left, then left again at the third narrow side street, **Takeshita-dori**. This is the shopping mecca for pre-teens and teenagers from all over the city and, increasingly, the world. The west end of Harajuku provides what they want: from tote bags to bomber jackets, from K-pop trinkets to mobile phone pouches with furry mascots. And Takeshita-dori is the epicentre of this enterprise.

If you need a breather, nearby **Togo Shrine** offers tranquillity and foliage. On the first and fourth Sundays of each month, this is the venue for one of Tokyo's best **flea markets**, offering antique kimonos, rustic bric-a-brac and assorted paraphernalia, often for knock-down prices (and remember, you can haggle here).

The quirky clothes stores and edgy design studios that once defined Harajuku can still be found in the back alleys – **Cat Street** on the south side of Omotesando is worth a detour – but they are gradually being edged out by the mainstream fashion houses and corporate brands.

From the Meiji-dori intersection, Omotesando becomes a broad boulevard lined with graceful zelkova trees. On the left you will pass **Omotesando Hills**, an upmarket shopping mall.

Shinjuku

In the Edo period, **Shinjuku** ㉜ was where two of the major highways from the west came together, and travellers would stop here to rest for the last leg of their journey to the capital. By the early 1900s, the area had become a sort of bohemian quarter, beloved of the city's filmmakers, writers, artists and

The teenage magnet that is Takeshita-dori

intellectuals. After World War II, it emerged as one of Tokyo's major transport hubs. About three million people pass through Shinjuku station every day. The station itself divides Shinjuku into two distinctly different areas, east and west.

West Shinjuku

West Shinjuku rejoices in a special gift of nature: relatively stable bedrock on which engineers can now erect earthquake-safe skyscrapers – foremost among them, the **Metropolitan Government Office** (North Observatory: Tue–Sun 9am–11pm, South Observatory: Wed–Mon 9.30am–5pm; free), better known as **City Hall**. The City Hall complex consists of a 48-storey main office building, a 34-storey annexe, the Metropolitan Assembly building and a central courtyard. The main building soars 243m (797ft), splitting on the 33rd floor into two towers. The observation decks on the 45th floors of both towers offer panoramic views.

At the western edge of Shinjuku (actually in the district called Honmachi) are Tokyo Opera City and the New National Theatre. Despite the names, these were not government projects but a private undertaking. The **New National Theatre** (10am–6pm; box office tel: 5352-9999; www.nntt.jac.go.jp), inaugurated in 1997, boasts a 1,810-seat opera house and two smaller performance spaces. **Opera City** (box office tel: 5353-9999; www.operacity.jp) is a 55-storey office tower, with a sunken garden, an art museum and a concert hall of lavish design.

Mount Takao

You don't have to leave the city to see hills and forest. Just 45 minutes by express train from Shinjuku on the Keio line, Takaosan-guchi station is the starting-off point for the trail up Mt Takao. It's not a hard hike to the Buddhist temple at the top (altitude 600m/2,000ft), and you'll never be alone, but it gives an idea of what rural Japan looks like.

East Shinjuku

East Shinjuku

East Shinjuku is really two places in one: a daytime quarter of department stores, vertical malls and discount stores, and a night-time quarter of bars (straight and gay), cheap restaurants, strip joints, game parlours, jazz clubs, rooms-by-the-hour hotels, and honky-tonks (with most of the last concentrated in a seedy, neon-lit neighbourhood called Kabuki-cho). Although the neighbourhood isn't visibly dangerous, it's all too easy for the unwary visitor to wander into a rip-off. If you plan to explore Kabuki-cho, do so with a knowledgeable local guide.

The two main avenues of East Shinjuku are Yasukuni-dori and Shinjuku-dori. Some 10 minutes' walk from the station on Yasukuni-dori, and a block north, is the **Hanazono-jinja**, a shrine built in the early Edo period. It was consecrated to Yamatotakeru no Mikoto, a warrior-hero whose exploits appear in the earliest (8th-century) compilations of Japanese legends.

A longer walk on Shinjuku-dori will bring you to the north end of **Shinjuku Gyoen National Garden**. Originally a feudal estate, the garden (a collection of gardens, really, in Japanese, French and English styles) became part of the imperial household after the Meiji restoration and, in 1949, a public

Shinjuku Gyoen
National Garden

park. There is also a botanical greenhouse. Shinjuku Gyoen is famous for its flowering cherry trees in April and for its chrysanthemums in the first two weeks of October.

BAYSIDE TOKYO

Tsukiji

In 1657 a fire broke out in Tokugawa Ieyasu's new capital. It burned for two days and destroyed about 70 percent of the city. In the course of rebuilding, a huge tract of land was reclaimed from the marshes east of Edo Castle and parcelled out for villas and temples. This was **Tsukiji**, which after 1853 became the site of Tokyo's first American and European settlement. However, except for a few memorial stones and monuments, nothing survives of the area's 19th-century history.

The sight to see today in this part of Tokyo is the **Tsukiji Central Wholesale Fish Market** ❸❸ (Mon–Sat, shops close around 1pm; closed hols and 2nd and 4th Wed of every month). The market starts early, but even if you arrive at 8 or 9am, there is plenty going on. Take the Hibiya subway line to Tsukiji and leave the station by the No. 2 exit. Across the avenue (Shin-Ohashi-dori) on your left is the Indian-style facade of **Tsukiji Hongan-ji Temple** ❸❹. Walk southwest on Shin-Ohashi-dori and cross the main intersection (Harumi-dori). Turn left at the next traffic light, walk to the end of the road, turn right – and you will find yourself in the orchestrated pandemonium of the world's largest fish market. Including the auction spaces, the market has a total area of about 22 hectares (54 acres). About 1,600 wholesale dealers do business here, supplying 90 percent of the fish consumed in Tokyo every day and employing some 15,000 people.

Most of what the market sells arrives at Tsukiji at night in refrigerated trucks, from fishing ports all over the country. The catch is laid out in covered sheds along the Sumida River and auctioned off to licensed wholesalers, who trundle their purchases back into the market in barrows for resale to the restaurant owners and retailers who start arriving at about 7am. Regretfully, the auction is now mostly closed to the public. Other restrictions on where the public can wander within the market are imminent. Note that there is water running here all the time to keep the floors clean, so take care not to damage your footwear. The present site has bags of atmosphere. Make the most of it, as it is scheduled to relocate in 2014.

Tsukiji Fish Market

Sumida River boats

The path to the left as you enter the garden leads to the ferry landing, where the boats depart for their journeys up the Sumida River to Asakusa (see box, page 42).

Hama Rikyu Detached Palace Garden

Return to Shin-Ohashi-dori and turn left. After a few minutes, the avenue brings you to an elevated walkway. The entrance to the **Hama Rikyu Detached Palace Garden** is on the left. Originally a Tokugawa family estate, the garden became a public park in 1945. In spite of the looming high-rise buildings of the nearby Shiodome complex, this is still a pleasant, relaxing green space, with woods and meadows, plus a traditional pavilion in the centre of a tidal pool.

Just opposite the Hama Rikyu Garden, the popular Shiodome complex is a sprawling waterfront development. The grove of skyscrapers includes the colossal **Caretta Shiodome** shopping mall and a large outdoor piazza for stylish al fresco coffees and meals.

Odaiba

Until recently, Tokyo turned its back on the bay on which it stands – cluttering its waterfront with ugly industrial sprawl and polluting the once-fertile waters. The creation of the **Odaiba** development on landfill islands symbolises a change of perspective. Connected to the mainland by the massive **Rainbow Bridge** ㉟ (the lights change colour at night), Odaiba is primarily a leisure area, and getting there is half the fun, by means of the futuristic, driverless Yurikamome elevated railway.

Once you get there you will find youth-oriented shopping malls, restaurants and game centres, two luxury hotels, the unmissable headquarters of the **Fuji TV** network (architect Kenzo Tange), the mind-expanding **National Museum of**

Emerging Science and Innovation, Palette Town, which includes a giant Ferris wheel, the **Mega Web** , Toyota's interactive car showroom, and **Venus Fort** and **Diver City**, two indoor malls. Another major attraction is the **Oedo Onsen Monogatari**, a complex of hot spring baths with a traditional Edo-era look. In winter Odaiba can be cold, windy and often empty. But on a sunny day, it is certainly worth exploring for anyone with an interest in contemporary Tokyo.

Sengaku-ji Temple

Few foreign visitors make it to **Sengaku-ji**, in the south of the city, but the temple has strong historical resonances for the Japanese. In 1701 Lord Asano, provoked into the serious transgression of drawing his sword at court, was ordered to commit *seppuku*, ritual disembowelment, making his retainers *ronin*

Hama Rikyu Detached Palace Garden

Rainbow Bridge connects Odaiba with the mainland

(masterless samurai). Smarting from the shame, 47 of the *ronin* plotted their revenge on Lord Kira, who had provoked Lord Asano. Breaking into his mansion two years later, they severed his head, took it through the snowy streets to Sengaku-ji and placed it on their master's grave. Reluctantly, the authorities ordered them to commit suicide, an incident much celebrated in kabuki plays, puppet dramas, TV and film. People still come to pay their respects at the graves, and to burn incense. A small museum in the temple grounds contains memorabilia and personal effects belonging to the *ronin*.

EXCURSIONS

Three easy-to-manage trips from Tokyo make a memorable addition to your visit, if time permits. One of them, to Kamakura, is a daytrip. The others, to Nikko and to Mt Fuji/Hakone, will be more enjoyable as overnighters.

Nikko

In the mountains of Tochigi Prefecture, **Nikko ③⑦** is about two hours north of Tokyo by train, either by JR or the cheaper Tobu lines. It is the final resting place of Ieyasu, founder of the Tokugawa shogunate, who died in 1616 and was declared a god – thereafter known in his apotheosis as Tosho Daigongen (the Great Incarnation Who Illuminates the East).

His sanctuary, **Toshogu-jinja**, is one of the two most important elements of the sites at Nikko (among the many buildings, look out for the famous woodcarving of the 'See, Speak and Hear No Evil' monkeys). The other is **Daiyu-in**, the memorial to Ieyasu's grandson Iemitsu, who actually built the complex. These monuments are utterly different from anything else you are likely to see in Japan, with Chinese-inspired architecture, intricately carved and painted, meant to impress the world with the Tokugawa wealth and power. They draw millions of visitors every year.

Other important buildings on the grounds here include Rinno-ji, a temple of the Tendai sect of Buddhism. Another is Futarasan, a Shinto shrine that is the most ancient place of worship at Toshogu, predating the Tokugawa dynasty and its works by some 900 years. In a forest of towering cedars, the site is one of the most impressive in Japan. The best time to visit is the third week of May or October, for the half-yearly Toshogu festivals. Some 1,200 parishioners of the shrine, in period costume, re-enact the procession that brought the remains of

Elaborate detail at the Toshogu-jinja complex

Looking through Kara-mon gate towards Yomei-mon gate at Toshogu-jinja

Tokugawa Ieyasu to his mausoleum in 1617. There is also a demonstration of *yabusame*, an ancient ritual contest of archery on horseback.

Higher in the mountains above the shrine complex is **Chuzen-ji** ㉛, a lake made aeons ago when a now-dormant volcano erupted and blocked the river courses, creating two waterfalls: Ryuzu (Dragon's Head) at one end and the impressive 97m (318ft) –high Kegon on the other. Famous for its rainbow trout, the waters of Chuzen-ji are too cold to swim in most of the year, but visitors throng to this area for its spectacular spring and autumn scenery and its numerous hot-springs resorts.

Kamakura

Less than an hour south of Tokyo by train, **Kamakura** ㉜ was the seat of the Kamakura shogunate, Japan's first military government, founded late in the 12th century after a long and bloody rivalry between two noble factions over control of the Imperial Court. The victorious Minamoto clan chose Kamakura as their headquarters because this fishing village was a great natural fortress, girded on three sides by steep, wooded hills. Here they created the Way of the Samurai: the values, codes, religion and culture of a warrior caste that would rule Japan for 700 years. Much of that culture was inspired by Zen Buddhism, its sense of discipline and self-control and its austere philosophy of art and life.

From the JR station at Kita (North) Kamakura, you can easily reach several of Kamakura's temples. **Engaku-ji**, for example, founded in 1282, was second in the group of influential Zen monasteries called the Five Mountains. It is Kamakura's largest temple complex, with 17 of the original 46 buildings. Nearby **Tokei-ji**, known as the Divorce Temple, was unique as a sanctuary for women of the warrior caste seeking to escape unhappy marriages. The Treasure House of Tokei-ji has an important collection of Kamakura-period art and calligraphy.

South of Tokei-ji, on the way to the city centre, are Meigetsu-in and Jochi-ji, Zen temples with especially fine gardens. Further south is Kencho-ji, an active monastery where visitors can take part in Zen meditation sessions.

In Kamakura proper, don't miss **Tsurugaoka Hachiman-gu**, the shrine complex built by Yoritomo no Minamoto, the first

The Great Buddha (Daibutsu), Kotoku-in Temple

Bamboo grove around
Hokokuji temple, Kamakura

Kamakura shogun. It was also probably Yoritomo's idea to create a seated Buddha for his capital to rival the bronze figure made in 749 for Todai-ji Temple in Nara. That idea bore fruit in 1292 with the casting of the 120-ton **Daibutsu** in the courtyard of Kotoku-in Temple – probably the most photographed image of Japan after Mt Fuji. Kotoku-in is in Hase, the district in the western part of Kamakura, where the other major attraction is **Hasedera**. In the Kannon hall of this temple is the largest wooden devotional figure in the country: a statue of the Eleven-Faced Goddess of Mercy, 10m (33ft) high, carved from a single tree trunk and covered in gold leaf. If you have time, take a ride down the coast on the Enoden Line (half train, half streetcar) to Enoshima, a beach resort.

Hakone and Mt Fuji

Hakone ④⓪ is a national park and resort area southeast of Mt Fuji, extremely popular with weekend visitors from Tokyo. Among its many attractions is the **Hakone Open-Air Museum**, with its remarkable collection of Western and Japanese sculpture, with works by such modern masters as Moore, Calder and Giacometti. Visitors stop here on the way to the little town of Gora to catch the cable car for a ride up into the mountains and across the smoking, volcanic Owaku Valley to the shore of Lake Ashi. Excursion cruisers leave from the piers at Togendai for Hakone-machi on the other side of the lake; on a good day, the reflection of Mt Fuji in these clear blue waters is breathtaking. In Hakone-machi you can view the Hakone Sekisho, an exact replica of a Tokugawa garrison checkpoint, with a small museum of period costumes and weapons. The surrounding area is known for its inns and thermal baths.

The ascent of **Mt Fuji** itself usually starts not at Lake Ashi but at Lake Kawaguchi, in the resort area further north. Climbers can take a bus from the lake to Go-gome ('Fifth Station') to begin the five-hour hike to the summit. Truly dedicated pilgrims start around midnight, reaching the top in time to greet the sunrise. There's no danger of losing the well-marked trail, and the night ascent obviates the need to stay at any of the dormitory-style mountain huts along the way, where accommodation is truly awful. Pack extra-warm clothing and wear good hiking boots, hats and gloves. The climbing season is in July and August.

Mt Fuji, Japan's iconic landmark

WHAT TO DO

ENTERTAINMENT AND NIGHTLIFE

Tokyo easily holds its own with such cities as New York and London as a performing arts venue. Audiences are appreciative and willing to buy expensive tickets, making it possible for promoters to bring in the top names in music, from rock and jazz to chamber orchestras and opera – and to support an enormous range of local talent as well. Cinema, too, thrives here, with arthouse films as well as Hollywood blockbusters.

Above all, a visit to Tokyo offers ample opportunity to sample Japan's own great native stage traditions: kabuki, *noh* and *bunraku*.

Kabuki. The best place to see kabuki is at the Kabuki-za (4-12-15 Ginza, Chuo-ku, tel: 5565-6000), renovated in 2012. Call by 6pm the day before a performance for reservations. There are two performances daily during the season: matinees run from 11am to about 3.30pm, evening performances from 4.30pm to around 9pm. If you prefer not to stay for an entire play (kabuki plots can be rather murky, and it's the spectacle that makes the event worth seeing), you can buy a very inexpensive unreserved ticket in the topmost gallery for just one act. If that whets your appetite, you can always buy another ticket.

Noh. *Noh* is a form of masked drama that is one of the sources of kabuki. Its origins date back to 14th-century performances at religious festivals, and it has remained virtually unchanged since then. Movement in *noh* is extremely slow and stylised; the language is poetic, further from modern Japanese than Shakespeare is from modern English. Even Japanese

Kabuki, a traditional theatre form, is on Unesco's intangible cultural heritage list audiences find it hard to follow. The plays in the *noh* repertoire are all written for only two actors. The roles are highly symbolic, all with their own conventional masks and (as in kabuki) specific costumes – heavy brocaded silk robes that are works of art in their own right.

There are three principal traditional schools of *noh* in Tokyo, presenting plays in their own theatres: the Kanze Noh-gakudo (1-16-4 Shoto, Shibuya-ku, tel: 3469-5241), the Hosho Noh-gakudo (1-5-9 Hongo, Bunkyo-ku, tel: 3811-4843) and the Umewaka Noh-gakuin (2-6-14 Higashi-Nakano, Nakano-ku, tel: 3363-7748). There are also performances at the National Noh Theatre (4-18-1 Sendagaya, Shibuya-ku, tel: 3423-1331) and the Cerulean Tower Noh Theatre (Cerulean Tower Tokyu Hotel, Floor B2, 26-1 Sakuragaoka-cho, Shibuya-ku; tel: 3477-6412). To get the full sense of mystery that a *noh* play is supposed to create, however, you should try to see one of the torchlit performances

Kabuki

Dating from the Edo period, kabuki, meaning 'cock-eyed' or 'out of the ordinary', is theatre with attitude. It was invented at the beginning of the 17th century by itinerant dancers (mostly women) who inspired near-riots for their sensual performances. The Tokugawa government clamped down on this new entertainment, but it remained by popular demand. There were swashbuckling dramas (*jidai-mono*), supernatural stories, domestic dramas (*sewa-mono*) and tragedies. Women were banned from taking part in 1629, but the male actors who take female roles have a seductive, dazzling femininity.

Going to the kabuki is still a major event. People bring their lunch to the theatre, stay all day and shout out the names of their favourite actors when they appear on stage. The actors themselves serve their apprenticeships for years within tightly-knit family organisations that trace their lineage back 12 generations or more.

called *takigi noh* held in the courtyards of temples, usually during the summer.

Bunraku. *Bunraku* puppet theatre is associated more with Osaka than Tokyo. It developed in the western part of Japan in the 18th century and has no theatre of its own here. The music and narrative in *bunraku* take some getting used to, but the puppets themselves are miraculous – half life-sized, so intricate and expressive that each one requires three people to operate. By convention, only the puppeteer who moves the head and right arm can be seen on stage; the other two wear black costumes and hoods and are supposed to be 'invisible'. There are occasional performances of *bunraku* in the small hall of the National Theatre (4-1 Hayabusa-cho, Chiyoda-ku, tel: 3265-7411). If there's one on the calendar during your visit, it's well worth seeing.

Geisha in traditional robes

Butoh. In the 1960s and early 1970s, Japanese experiments in avant-garde theatre and dance gave birth to a new genre called *butoh*, which soon became known worldwide. To the uninitiated, *butoh* is grotesque in the extreme. Dancers perform in rags or nearly naked; they shave their heads and paint their bodies white; the movements are contorted, violent, disturbingly erotic. *Butoh* companies are not as active now in Tokyo as they once were, but the occasional performance is worth looking out for.

Listings magazines

The best source in English for music, film and theatre in Tokyo is the online magazine *Tokyo Q* (www.tokyoq.com). The free weekly magazine *Metropolis* (available in many bars and bookshops) has good listings too.

Music and Opera

During the 1970s and 1980s, **classical music** benefited greatly from a burst of concert hall building. Among the venues hosting full-scale symphony orchestras are Suntory Hall (1-13-1 Akasaka, Minato-ku, tel: 3505-1001), NHK Hall (2-2-1 Jinnan, Shibuya-ku, Tokyo; tel: 3465-1751) and Orchard Hall (Tokyu Bunkamura, 2-24-1 Dogenzaka, Shibuya-ku, tel: 3477-9999). **Opera** in Tokyo long languished without a venue. The New National Theatre and Tokyo Opera City Concert Hall (3-20-2 Nishi-Shinjuku, Shinjuku-ku, tel: 5353-0788 or 5351-3011) have remedied that situation (see page 70).

The major venues for **rock and pop** concerts in Tokyo are the 56,000-seat Tokyo Dome (1-3-61 Koraku, Bunkyo-ku, tel: 3811-2111), Nakano Sun Plaza (4-1-1 Nakano, Nakano-ku, tel: 3388-1151) and Nippon Budokan (2-3 Kita-no-maru Koen, Chiyoda-ku, tel: 3216-5100).

Nightlife

Tokyo likes to party as hard as it works, and the variety of nightlife is astonishing. There are clubs and bars of all descriptions in every part of town, ranging from sleek, exclusive salons to simple, friendly hole-in-the-wall counters. And when it comes to music, you can find virtually any genre – jazz, reggae, salsa, or techno – either live or via DJs.

For most visitors to Tokyo, the place to start is Roppongi. Whether it's ale and football at **The Hobgoblin** (3-16-33 Roppongi, Minato-ku, tel: 3568-1280), lager and lechery at **Gas Panic** (3-15-24 Roppongi, Minato-ku, tel: 3405-0633) or cigars and premium tequila at **Agave** (7-15-10 Roppongi, Minato-ku, tel: 3497-0229), there is lubrication to suit all tastes. If you want to listen to smooth music and have a drink at the same time, the bands at **STB 139** (6-7-11 Roppongi, Minato-ku, tel: 5474-1395) play jazz and jazz-rock fusion, while **Billboard Live Tokyo** (Tokyo Midtown, 9-7-4 Akasaka, Minato-ku, tel: 3405-1133) hosts acts ranging from R&B to soul to light rock. And there's always something interesting going on at the **Super Deluxe** (3-1-25 Roppongi, Minato-ku, tel: 5412-0515), be it guerrilla theatre, hip designers, architectural presentations, *butoh* dance or industrial heavy metal bands.

Down the hill in Nishi-Azabu is **Muse** (B1 FL, 4-1-1 Nishi-Azabu, Minato-ku, tel: 5467-1188), an underground club with a funky vibe and a friendly crowd.

Visitors who like jazz should head for the Aoyama district. **Blue Note Tokyo** (6-3-16 Minami-Aoyama, Minato-ku, tel: 5485-0088) and **Body & Soul** (6-13-9 Minami-Aoyama,

Live music at Super Deluxe

Minato-ku, tel: 5466-3348) are intimate venues that draw leading musicians from all around the world, as does **B-Flat** (6-6-4 Akasaka, Minato-ku, tel: 5563-2563).

In general, Akasaka and Ginza are more sedate areas, where entertaining on the expense account is done at cabarets, nightclubs and exclusive 'hostess clubs'. At the other extreme, Shibuya offers inexpensive pubs, cinemas and live music spots, catering mainly to students and young professionals. It also has a vibrant clubbing scene, with many venues running from late at night until dawn. Three of the best are **Ruby Room** (2-25-17 Dogenzaka, Shibuya-ku, tel: 3780-3022), **Vision** (2-10-7 Dogenzaka, Shibuya-ku, tel: 03-5728-2824) and the massive **Womb** (2-16 Maruyama-cho, Shibuya-ku, tel: 5459-0039).

And then there is Shinjuku, the anything-goes nightlife quarter, good for bars (straight, gay, transvestite, S&M), peep shows, game parlours and general carousing. While Kabuki-cho is not overtly dangerous, you should watch out for pickpockets and clip joints that don't have their drinks prices posted.

If you're in Tokyo during the heat of summer, beer halls make a welcome addition to the nightlife. Some of these, like Sapporo's marvellous retro **Beer Hall Lion** (7-9-20 Ginza, Chuo-ku, tel: 3571-2590) operate year-round indoors. But

Karaoke

Karaoke is Japan's favourite pastime, and Tokyo offers abundant opportunities to get behind the mic. As is happening increasingly in the West, karaoke in Japan is done in private rooms with groups of friends or co-workers. Most venues offer a playlist of thousands of songs, as well as a large menu of food and drink. Two popular spots are Shidax Village in Shibuya (1-12-3 Jinnan, Shibuya-ku, tel: 3461-9356) and Lovenet in Roppongi (Hotel Ibis 3-4 FL, 7-14-4 Roppongi, Minato-ku, tel: 5771-5511); the latter offers rooms with themes like 'Candy' and 'Morocco'.

during the summer, you will also find rooftop beer gardens on the upper levels of department stores and hotel gardens across the city.

FESTIVALS

Religious observances, or *matsuri*, are held at Shinto shrines. The deities of a shrine are carried through the streets in palanquins by dancing, swaying, chanting parishioners, to the music of flutes and drums. The three biggest, loudest and most exuberant shrine festivals in Tokyo are the Sanno Matsuri, the Sanja Matsuri and the Kanda Matsuri (see page 97).

Discover the nightlife by starting in Roppongi

Solemn observances take place on New Year's Day, when people visit shrines, such as Meiji-jingu, and temples, including Senso-ji, to pray for good fortune and health in the year to come. Also solemn is All Souls (*O-bon*), when the spirits of one's ancestors are believed to return for a brief visit to the family Buddhist altar. The latter coincides roughly with another of Tokyo's great blow outs: the Fireworks Festival on the Sumida River, which is an event not to be missed.

SPORTS

Casual visitors to Tokyo will find very few opportunities for recreational sports. A smattering of private clubs have squash and racquetball courts, but if they're open to non-members it will be at fees you're unlikely to want to pay. Public tennis courts are equally hard to find and are usually reserved weeks in advance. Tokyo has a fair number of meshed-in golf driving ranges, like the famous three-tiered facility in Shiba-Koen, next door to Zojo-ji temple; for information about playing a round at a local course, check the comprehensive Golfjin website (www.golfjin.com). Travellers serious about keeping in shape should consider staying at one of the major international hotels, which have fitness centres and swimming pools.

Joggers have no problems. The most favoured run in Tokyo is around the Imperial Palace grounds, a distance

The Art and Culture of Sumo

Wrestlers square off in a dirt ring about 4.5m (15ft) in diameter and charge straight at one another. The first to step out of the ring or touch the ground with anything but the soles of his feet loses. Contestants may not hit below the belt, strike with the closed fist or pull each other's hair; otherwise, anything goes. There are no weight limits.

Tournaments and exhibitions are held in different parts of the country at different times, but the 'stables' are in Tokyo. Every sumo wrestler belongs to a stable – called a *beya* – owned by a retired wrestler. Most stables are in the Asakusabashi and Ryogoku areas, on both sides of the Sumida River, in walking distance of the Kokugikan. Tournaments are in January, May and September, and you can see wrestlers on the streets, in their wooden clogs and kimonos. Fans will go to their favourite stables between 7am and 11am to watch practice sessions.

Artefacts related to the sport, its history and rituals are displayed at the **Sumo Museum** in the Ryogoku Kokugikan (1-3-28 Yoko-ami, Sumida-ku, tel: 3622-0366; Mon–Fri 10am–4.30pm; free; www.sumo. or.jp/eng/museum) see page 47.

Sumo tournament at Ryogoku Kokugikan

of nearly 5km (3 miles) with a challenging uphill section. You won't lack for company: local diehards are out on this course from first light to dark, in any imaginable weather. By some solemn unwritten convention, you're supposed to start at the Sakurada-mon Gate and follow the moat clockwise.

Sumo wrestling. If you're in Tokyo during a tournament, you really ought to spend an afternoon at the Kokugikan – the National Sumo Stadium (Ryogoku Kokugikan, 1-3-28 Yokoami, Sumida-ku, tel: 3623-5111), on the east bank of the Sumida River in Ryogoku – to watch the wrestling. Tournaments are held in early January, in mid-May and in mid-September.

Sumo wrestling is an ancient religious rite; anyone watching a match for the first time will not hesitate to grant it the status of a performing art. It's a great show, and the Tokyo tournaments are not to be missed.

SHOPPING

What to buy in Tokyo? Electronics spring to mind – but it's not at all certain that you will find substantially better buys than at home. On the other hand, you will find more variety and more reasonable prices locally for the fashions of Japanese couturiers like Issey Miyake, Kawakubo Rei and Hanae Mori. Look for them in the boutiques of the Aoyama and Omotesando areas, and in the designer sections of such department stores as Takashimaya and Matsuya. Better yet, focus on things traditionally Japanese in the craft sections of most department stores and in the following speciality shops.

Ceramics. Pottery-making began in Japan some 12,000 years ago. The various styles best known today (Seto, Bizen, Mino, Shigaraki, Raku, and Kutani) emerged in the 15th and 16th centuries. Again, department stores all carry good selections.

Dolls. Dolls in Japan are not so much toys as decorative and ceremonial objects. They come in many different styles and materials. The best selection is at Kyugetsu (1-20-4 Yanagibashi, Taito-ku, tel: 3861-5511).

Perfect prints

Sakai Kokodo (1-2-14 Yurakucho, Chiyoda-ku, tel: 3591-4678), close to the Imperial Hotel in Hibiya, is the best place to look for Edo-era woodblock prints. This small gallery stocks exquisite (and expensive) *ukiyo-e* by Hiroshige and Hokkusai, as well as a range of reasonably priced reproductions.

Kimonos. Formal kimonos are dyed silk and brocade – and very expensive. You can find them second-hand at flea markets in the ¥10,000 range, but a more practical choice would be a cotton summer kimono (*yukata*), stencil-dyed in a handsome traditional blue-and-white design, for about ¥8,000. Look for these in shops and stalls along the arcades of

Asakusa, around Senso-ji Temple.

Lacquerware. Lacquerware needs a humid climate to keep the wood underneath the resin from shrinking. That's a bonus for visitors: the less expensive pieces – no less beautiful – have plastic bases, making them safer to bring home. Most department stores carry a large selection.

Paper. Papermaking from various plant fibres is another ancient tradition in Japan. The paper (*washi*), wonderfully soft and highly durable, lends itself to the crafting of a wide variety of useful and decorative objects – and you couldn't ask for anything lighter or less breakable to

Recreate the tea ceremony after your holiday with a souvenir

take home. Two shops worth visiting are Itoya (2-7-15 Ginza, Chuo-ku, tel: 3561-8311) and Kyokyodo (5-7-4 Ginza, Chuo-ku, tel: 3571-4429). At Origami Kaikan (1-7-14 Yushima, Bunkyo-ku, tel: 3811-4025) you can also tour a papermaking workshop.

Pearls. Since the technique of producing cultured pearls was developed here in 1893, Japan has been the place to buy these remarkable gems. Pearls are a substantial investment. If you are not already a knowledgeable judge of quality-for-price, you should shop for them at one of the reputable dealers, such as Mikimoto (4-5-5 Ginza, Chuo-ku, tel: 3535-4611) or Tasaki (5-7-5 Ginza, Minato-ku, tel: 3289-1111), to be sure you are getting your money's worth.

Shopping for crafts. Three locations offer excellent one-stop shopping for all the craft items above, and more. Japan Traditional Crafts Aoyama Square (8-1-22 Akasaka, Minato-ku, tel: 5785-1001) certifies and sells craftworks of outstanding quality from all over Japan. The Oriental Bazaar (5-9-13 Jingumae, Shibuya-ku, tel: 3400-3933; closed Thur) carries art and antiques as well as crafts, plus souvenirs of Chinese and Korean origin, all at reasonable prices. The International Shopping Arcade (1-7-3 Uchisaiwai-cho, Chiyoda-ku) is a gallery of duty-free shops near the Imperial Hotel; available here are cameras, electronics and pearls as well as craft souvenirs.

Department Stores

A few hours in a Tokyo department store can be a revelation. First, there is the exquisite politeness of the staff. Then there are prepared foods and gourmet speciality departments on the lower levels, with picture-perfect displays – and stupefying prices. Many of the food stalls have small samples out on the counter. Nibble as you explore; no one will object. All department stores have reasonably priced restaurants and coffee shops on the upper floors. And then there are the galleries. Department stores, especially those in Ginza and Nihonbashi, promote themselves extensively as cultural institutions. The exhibits they sponsor, in cooperation with major collections abroad,

Major stores

Isetan 3-14-1 Shinjuku, Shinjuku-ku.
Keio 1-1-4 Nishi-Shinjuku, Shinjuku-ku.
Matsuya 3-6-1 Ginza, Chuo-ku.
Matsuzakaya 6-10-1 Ginza, Chuo-ku.
Mitsukoshi 4-6-16 Ginza, Chuo-ku.
Parco 13-11 Udagawa-cho, Shibuya-ku.
Seibu 1-28-1 Minami-ike-bukuro, Toshima-ku.
Takashimaya 2-4-1 Nihon-bashi, Chuo-ku.
Wako 4-14-11 Ginza, Chuo-ku.

often put the city's public art museums to shame.

Stores accept most major credit cards and will ship your purchases home. Some staff speak English. Stores close one or two days a month (different stores on different days of the week), but normally on Tuesdays or Wednesdays. Hours are 10am or 11am to 7pm or 8pm.

CHILDREN'S TOKYO

There is no scarcity of places to take children, but good weather on weekends brings out like-minded Japanese families in big numbers. Be prepared for long queues.

The Prada shop in Aoyama is an architectural landmark

Tokyo Dome City. This mixed-use theme park has a giant roller-coaster and the world's first hubless Ferris wheel. It's a short walk from the Korakuen stop on the Marunouchi subway line. Open daily 10am–8pm; admission ¥1,500 before 6pm, ¥1,800 thereafter.

Tokyo Disneyland. Except for signs and some of the food, there's little to distinguish the Tokyo version of Disneyland from its parent enterprise in California. Take the Tozai line from Nihonbashi to Urayasu, then the park bus to the gate; you can also take the JR Keiyo line from Tokyo station to Maihama and walk to the entrance. Buy tickets in advance at the Disneyland booth in Tokyo station, near the Yaesu

Theme park ride at Tokyo Dome city

North exit. Open Mon–Fri 9am–9pm, Sat–Sun and hols 8am–10pm, earlier hours in summer; one-day passport ¥6,200, evening only ¥3,300. The themes at DisneySea, an amusement complex next door, are all water-based.

Toshima-en. This amusement park in northwest Tokyo has four roller-coasters, seven swimming pools – and an original carousel from New York City's Coney Island. Take the Marunouchi subway line from Tokyo station to Ikebukuro and change to the Seibu Ikebukuro line to the park. (3-25-1 Mukoyama, Nerima-ku, tel: 3990-8800; Thur–Mon 10am–6pm, daily mid-July–mid-Aug; admission ¥1,000, children aged under 12, ¥500; one-day pass ¥3,900, children ¥2,900.)

Tama Dobutsu-Koen (Tama Zoo). In this wildlife park in western Tokyo, animals roam freely, separated from visitors by a system of moats. Take a Keio line train for Takao from Shinjuku and change at Takahata-Fudo station. (7-1-1 Hodokubo, Hino-shi, tel: 042-591-1611; Thur–Tue 9.30am–5pm, tickets sold until 4pm; adults ¥600, students (13–15) ¥200; free admission on 5 May, 29 Apr and 1 Oct.)

Shinagawa Suizokukan. Tokyo's small, well-designed aquarium has a walk-through glass tunnel. There are dolphin and sea lion shows throughout the day. Take the Keihin-Kyuko line local train from Shinagawa to Omori-kaigan; follow the ceramic fish on the pavement to the aquarium. (Shinagawa Kumin Park, 3-2-1 Katsushima, Shinagawa-ku, tel: 3762-3433; Wed–Mon 10am–5pm, doors close at 4.30pm; admission ¥1,300, under-16s ¥600, under-5s ¥300.)

Calendar of Events

1–3 January New Year's visits to major shrines and temples.

2 January Reception of the public by Imperial Family on Palace grounds.

6 January Parade of traditional fire-fighters in Harumi.

Mid-January First sumo tournament of the year (for 15 days at the Kokugikan sumo stadium).

3 February Setsubun (last day of winter) festival involves bean-throwing ceremonies at major shrines and temples.

Late March/early April Cherry blossoms at their peak in Ueno Park and around the Palace.

17 April Ceremonial music and dance at Toshogu shrine in Ueno.

21–23 April Spring festival at Yasukuni shrine.

5 May Annual festival at the Suitengu shrine.

Mid-May Sumo tournament (15 days at Kokugikan sumo stadium).

Mid-May (weekend before 14–15 May, odd-numbered years) Kanda Matsuri at the Kanda Myojin shrine, with festive processions.

Late May (3rd Friday, Saturday and Sunday) Sanja Matsuri: vivid, boisterous processions starting from the Asakusa-jinja shrine and winding through the surrounding streets. Also traditional dancing and music.

10–16 June (in even-numbered years) Sanno Matsuri at the Sanno Hie-jinja shrine in Akasaka, with festive procession past the Imperial Palace and in Ginza.

Late June Irises in bloom in Meiji-jingu.

July Sumida River fireworks festival (last Saturday of the month).

13–16 August O-bon (All Souls) dances held at various locations.

Mid-September 15-day sumo tournament at Kokugikan stadium.

17–19 October Autumn festival at Yasukuni shrine.

18 October Asakusa Kannon Matsuri at Senso-ji temple.

31 October–3 November Annual festival at Meiji shrine.

November Tori no Ichi festival at Otori-jinja near Asakusa (date varies).

15 November (and weekends on either side) Shichi-go-san: children aged seven, five or three dress in kimonos and receive special blessings.

31 December Joya-no-kane: bells toll 108 strokes at Buddhist temples.

EATING OUT

Tokyo is a city geared to the needs of literally millions of people who dine out after work with colleagues or clients before they go home. By some counts, there are more than 200,000 establishments here licensed to sell food and drink, from humble street stalls to elegant restaurants with celebrity chefs. But the eating culture isn't just focused on quantity; Tokyo consistently ranks among one of the top cities in the world for the quality of its restaurants. The city also has the largest wholesale fish market in Asia (see page 72), and seafood in all its varieties takes pride of place on menus all over town.

Above all, Tokyo is a great cosmopolitan capital, and the legendary Japanese hospitality to ideas from elsewhere applies also to food. European, Asian, Middle Eastern, Latin American

Japanese noodles are made from wheat or buckwheat

– there's at least one restaurant somewhere in Tokyo for virtually every cuisine you can imagine. You might not always find a menu in English, but most popular-priced eateries make up for that omission with pictures or plastic models of the food they serve, displayed in window cases. Best of all, the food in Tokyo is safe wherever you go.

Where to Eat

As a general rule, the foods of other cultures are at their best and most authentic uptown, in Ginza, Akasaka, Roppongi, Hiroo, Ebisu and Daikanyama. In Shibuya, Harajuku and Shinjuku, foreign restaurants tend to market themselves to students and young office workers. Prices are lower, but the food often leaves something to be desired. As you go north and east into Shitamachi, you'll find the inexpensive family restaurants serving things traditionally Japanese. Sushi bars in Tsukiji tend to have the freshest ingredients and serve the biggest portions. Nihonbashi, Asakusa and the surrounding 'downtown' quarters are known especially for tempura and eel restaurants, but good tempura can be found everywhere in the city.

International hotels in Tokyo make a practice of inviting in branch operations of star-quality restaurants (the Tour d'Argent, for example, at the New Otani), and thus have some of the city's best cuisine, both Western and Japanese. Department stores and high-rise office buildings have whole floors of inexpensive restaurants and snack bars. They tend to be crowded – and the Western-style fast-food operations should be avoided – but otherwise these are good places to

Bento lunch boxes

break for lunch during your explorations of the city.

Restaurant hours and taxes. Tokyo dines early, and it is not uncommon for kitchens to shut down at 10pm or even earlier. However, many pub-style places, noodle shops and snack bars tend to stay open at least until midnight. A 5 percent national consumption tax is added to all restaurant bills. Another 5 percent local tax is added if the bill exceeds ¥7,500. At more expensive Western-style restaurants, a 10 percent or 15 percent service charge is often added as well. Tipping is not necessary.

What to Eat

Japanese cuisine. When it comes to Japanese food, even in simple restaurants, the quality is remarkable; in the best places, it is exceptional. Traditional cooking relies very little on sauces, spices or elaborate preparations. The emphasis is instead on fresh ingredients (vegetables, fish, seafood) and on the aesthetics of presentation. The seasons are important, but not only for the kinds of food that each one brings. Every season calls for different colours, shapes and textures in the tableware on which the food is served.

Flavouring is achieved mainly with soy sauce, bean paste (*miso*), sweet rice wine, horseradish (*wasabi*), ginger, scallions and (in some dishes) cayenne pepper. Fish is most often grilled, or it is served raw as *sashimi*. Other dishes are typically boiled or deep-fried in batter.

Full-course meals include soup and rice, usually served at the end. A typical soup is made with *miso* and often flavoured with littleneck clams. The Japanese make a great variety of pickles, which are served as garnishes or side dishes.

Noodle dishes are very popular in Japan, for lunch or for a quick meal on the run. Japanese wheat *(udon)* or buckwheat *(soba)* noodles can be served either hot or cold, accompanied by shrimp or vegetable tempura. Chinese noodles, called *ramen*, are served hot in a strongly flavoured meat-stock broth.

Perfection on a Plate

The most elegant genre of Japanese cooking is known as *kaiseki*, a procession of skilfully prepared dishes served in elegant surroundings on graceful ceramics and lacquerware. In *kaiseki*, balance is the key – not just of ingredients and flavours, but of colour, texture, temperature and presentation. The variety of cooking on display in a *kaiseki* meal is astonishing. A single dinner can include dishes that have been chilled, steamed, simmered, grilled, seared, stewed, and deep-fried, all prepared with ingredients chosen strictly for their freshness and seasonality.

Kaiseki meals are best enjoyed at inn-like restaurants known as *ryotei*. These eateries are divided into a number of small, private dining rooms with *tatami* mats on the floors – and, preferably, a garden view. The emphasis here is on privacy and discreetly professional service. Each room has an alcove, called a *tokonoma*, where there is always a hanging scroll or a flower arrangement to fit the season or the mood of the occasion. One or more of the staff, dressed in a kimono, attends exclusively to each room to serve the many dishes that comprise the meal, pour the sake, and make light conversation.

Kaiseki is certain to be more expensive at a *ryotei* than an ordinary restaurant, but well worth experiencing. Alas, there are fewer and fewer *ryotei* in Tokyo. Those that have survived the relentless modernisation of taste are for the most part in Akasaka, Tsukiji, Asakusa, Yanagibashi and Shimbashi.

Buckwheat (*soba*) noodle dish

In winter, the Japanese have a wide variety of one-pot meals (*nabe ryori*); the main ingredients can be thin slices of beef, crab, shellfish or chicken, added to a broth with Chinese cabbage, leeks, rice noodles and shiitake mushrooms. This is the ultimate social meal – the pot sits in the middle of the table and everyone takes a bit from it for his or her own bowl.

International cuisine. Tokyo is experiencing a love affair with French cuisine, with high-end restaurants and bistro-style eateries alike sprouting up in many neighbourhoods. This trend has been boosted by a boom in the wine market. Good wines from around the world are now available in Tokyo supermarkets and speciality shops. Consumers are learning about wine, and restaurants have expanded their lists accordingly. Unfortunately, this newfound popularity has not translated into lower prices; be prepared to pay dearly for decent wine in Tokyo.

Local diners have also been blessed with recent opportunities to experience the range and virtuosity of Italian cuisine.

Aspiring chefs who once thought only of France are now travelling to Italy and returning with authentic recipes.

The Indian restaurants in Tokyo are consistently good and relatively inexpensive. Some, established before World War II, are among the oldest 'ethnic' restaurants in the city. Chinese food is also good, but the typical neighbourhood version (called *chuka ryori*) is limited, much modified to suit Japanese tastes. For the real thing, seek out the Tokyo branch of one of the serious Chinatown restaurants in Yokohama.

Finally, don't ignore the dining benefits conferred by Tokyo's very large Korean population. At a Korean barbecue restaurant, you cook thin slices of beef fillet, brisket and raw vegetables on a gas-fired grill at your own table. Besides the many informal, inexpensive places, there are now many upmarket restaurants serving Korean cuisine of considerable refinement.

You won't need to dress up for dinner at most restaurants. Only such places as the French and Continental restaurants in the international hotels will insist on jackets and ties. Otherwise, go formal only if you feel like it. For Japanese-style restaurants with *tatami* seating, choose clothing you'll be comfortable in for a few hours with your legs gathered under you.

What to Drink

Sake. The perfect accompaniment to a Japanese meal is sake (Japanese rice wine) although the term 'wine' is probably a misnomer. The process of making sake might be considered closer to brewing than fermentation, as the milled rice is malted, steamed and mixed with water. Sake can be either sweet or dry, with subtle hints of other flavours. Traditionally, sake is brewed

> **Have a good slurp**
>
> A certain amount of noise is expected when you eat noodle dishes like *soba* and *ramen*. It's not impolite to slurp.

in winter, and it is at its best served fresh (it doesn't improve with age) with *sashimi* or other seafood.

The history of sake appears to have begun with the cultivation of rice itself, as early as 2,000 years ago. Originally, it was not merely a convivial (and potent) drink but also an offering to the gods, and it remains an essential part of Shinto rituals and many other traditional ceremonies.

Today there are roughly 3,000 sake makers, including a handful of mass-market operations that produce year-round. But there are still many smaller, regional

Casks of sake

enterprises that take enormous pride in their traditional craftsmanship and the distinctive local character of their products. Known as *jizake* (local brews), these connoisseur sake brands from regional breweries can now be found at many liquor shops, sake bars (known as *izakaya*) and restaurants in Tokyo.

Sake is generally clear in colour, and the taste can range from sharply dry to cloyingly sweet. In the finest varieties, the rice is polished to less than half its original weight. To produce this sake – known as *ginjo-shu* or *dai* (great) *ginjo*, depending on how much of the rice is milled – specialised yeasts are added in the brewing process to develop remarkable flavour profiles.

Because the delicate nuances of flavour are easily destroyed by heat, this top-grade sake is generally stored and served chilled. Top Japanese restaurants such as Kozue (see page 113) make a point of sourcing an elite selection of *ginjo-shu* from around the country. A more affordable way of sampling sake is to visit a specialist bar or *izakaya*; some stock 100 varieties or more.

Some good specialist bars are: Akaoni (2-15-3 Sangenjaya, Setagaya-ku, tel: 3410-9918, www.akaoni39.com), Buchi (9-7 Shinsencho, Shibuya-ku, tel: 5728-2085, www.to-vi.jp/buchi), Sake no Ana (3-5-8 Ginza, Chuo-ku, tel: 3567-1133, www.sakenoana.com), Sasagin (1-32-15 Uehara, Shibuya-ku, tel: 5454-3715) and Sasashu (2-2-6 Ikebukuro, Toshima-ku, tel: 3971-6796).

Beer. The history of beer-making in Japan goes back well over 100 years. Although the offerings of the four top mass-market brands (Sapporo, Asahi, Kirin and Ebisu) are predictably staid, a recent infatuation with craft brews has livened up Tokyo's beer scene.

Small breweries across the country have introduced an astonishing range of beers, ales, porters, weitzens, altbiers, pilsners, dunkels and stouts. Tokyo even has a couple of brewpubs, including T.Y. Harbor Brewing Co. (see page 113), which also serves excellent food. Beer-focused pubs include The Aldgate (30-4 Udagawa-cho, Shibuya-ku, tel: 3462-2983, www.the-aldgate.com), Popeye Beer Club (2-18-7 Ryogoku, Sumida-ku, tel: 3633-2120), Nakameguro Taproom (2-1-3 Kamimeguro, Meguro-ku, tel: 5768-3025, http://bairdbeer.com) and Ant 'N Bee (5-1-5 Roppongi, Minato-kuu, tel: 3478-1250).

Other drinks. *Shochu* has become a very fashionable drink. Much stronger than sake, with an alcohol content that starts at 25 percent, this distilled drink is made from potatoes, rice, barley or sugar. *Awamori* is an even stronger drink made from Thai rice, which hails from the southern islands of Okinawa.

TO HELP YOU ORDER...

A table for one/two please.	**hitori/futari desu ga, teeburu ga arimasu ku.**
How much is that?	**ikura desu ka**
The bill, please	**okanjoo onegai shimasu**
I would like ...	**... ga hoshiin desu ga**

... AND READ THE MENU

fish	**sakana**	grilled fish	**yaki zakana**
beef	**gyuu niku**	minced beef and vegetables	**sukiyaki**
pork	**buta niku**	buckwheat noodles	**soba**
chicken	**tori niku**		
duck	**kamo**	wheat noodles	**udon**
bread	**pan**		
potatoes	**poteto/ jagaimo**	battered fish and veg in noodle broth	**tempura soba/udon**
rice	**gohan**		
salad	**sarada**	Chinese noodles in stock	**ramen**
pickled vegetables	**tsukemono**		
fruit	**furuutsu/ kudamono**	savoury pancakes	**okonomiyaki**
vegetable	**yasai**		
pepper	**kosho**	tofu	**tofu**
salt	**shio**	tuna	**maguro**
sugar	**satoo**	salmon	**sake**
water	**mizu**	prawns	**ebi**
coffee	**koohii**	squid	**ika**
tea	**koocha**	raw fish with soy and wasabi	**sashimi**
wine	**wain**		
beer	**biiru**		
sake	**nihonshu**	rice balls with raw fish	**sushi**
miso soup	**misoshiro**		

PLACES TO EAT

For a three-course dinner per person, excluding drinks and taxes:

¥¥¥¥ *over ¥5,000*   ¥¥¥ *¥3,000–5,000*
¥¥ *¥2,000–3,000*   ¥ *under ¥2,000*

NIHOMBASHI/MARUNOUCHI/ YURAKUCHO/GINZA

Bird Land ¥¥¥ *Tsukamoto Sozan Bldg B1F, 4-2-15 Ginza, Chuo-ku, tel: 5250-1081, http://ginza-birdland.sakura.ne.jp.* Bird Land's master, Toshihiro Wada, was one of the first to match premium charcoal-grilled *yakitori* with wine. Start with his liver pâté, sample some sashimi breast meat and then try his superb *sansai-yaki* (grilled with Japanese pepper). It's all made from free-range chicken, it's all brilliant. Reservations essential.

Dhaba India ¥¥ *2-7-9 Yaesu, Chuo-ku, tel: 3272-7160, www.dhaba india.com.* Southern Indian food is hard to find in Tokyo, but this unpretentious place, just a block from Kyobashi station, hits the spot. The curries are rich, the *thali* meals are great value, and the masala *dhosas* delectable.

Oshima ¥¥¥¥ *Ginza Core Bldg 9F, 5-8-20 Ginza, Chuo-ku, tel: 3574-8080.* The seafood cuisine of Kanazawa, a city on the Sea of Japan, is served just steps from the main Ginza intersection. The setting is elegant, the service spot-on; the *jibuni* (a kind of casserole of duck and potatoes) and the grilled fresh yellowtail are out of this world. Open daily for lunch and dinner. Reservations advised.

Peter ¥¥¥¥ *The Peninsula Tokyo 24F, 1-8-1 Yurakucho, Chiyoda-ku, tel: 6270-2763.* A private lift whisks diners up to the Peninsula Tokyo's daring flagship restaurant. The kitchen is overseen by Patrice Matrineau, formerly chef de cuisine at the esteemed New York eatery *Daniel*. He delivers continental-inspired cooking with modern touches and the best local meats, seafood and produce.

Tapas Molecular Bar ¥¥¥ *Mandarin Oriental Tokyo 34F, 2-1-1 Nihombashi-Muromachi, Chuo-ku, tel: 3270-8188.* With dishes named 'Beach', 'Smoke', and 'Olive Oil Gummy', the Tapas Molecular Bar is Tokyo's leading outpost of avant-garde cuisine. This counter restaurant seats just eight diners at a time, and the experience – which can include as many as 20 courses in one meal – is equal parts gastronomy and performance art. The show starts at 6pm and 8.30pm nightly.

Ten-Ichi ¥¥¥ *6-6-5 Ginza, Chuo-ku, tel: 3571-1949, www.tenichi. co.jp.* One of Tokyo's top tempura restaurants, Ten-Ichi has become a Ginza institution. The batter-fried morsels of fish and vegetables are cooked in front of your eyes. If you can't get in here, there are many other branches, all reliable. A cheaper, more informal version, Ten-Ichi Deux can be found on the first floor of the nearby Nishi Ginza Depato building.

ASAKUSA/KAPPABASHI/UENO/AKIHABARA

Tatsumiya ¥¥ *1-33-5 Asakusa, Taito-ku, tel: 3842-7373.* A charming *ryotei* (traditional inn, with private dining rooms), Tatsumiya offers a special seven-course meal for foreign visitors (with *sashimi*, tofu and grilled chicken) at a very reasonable price. Located one block west of Asakusa station. Closed Monday. No credit cards.

Yabu Soba ¥ *2-10 Kanda-Awajicho, Chiyoda-ku, tel: 3251-0287, www. yabusoba.net.* Tokyo's most famous noodle restaurant is housed in a traditional wooden building behind the Kanda post office. The speciality is *soba*, buckwheat noodles served hot or cold. Try the *kamo-nanban* (in hot soup with duck) or *tempura seiro* (cold, with deep-fried prawns).

YAMANOTE (AKASAKA/AOYAMA/ HARAJUKU/SHINJUKU)

Hantei ¥¥¥ *2-12-15 Nezu, Bunkyo-ku, tel: 3828-1440.* Set in a handsome old wooden town house in a historic part of town, Hantei serves *kushi-age* – bite-sized morsels of fish, meat and vegetables breaded and deep-fried on sticks. There's no need to order: they just bring course after course until you tell them to stop. Located on Shinobazu-dori opposite Nezu station. No reservations taken.

Heichinrou ¥¥¥ *Sanno Park Tower 27F, 2-11-1 Nagata-cho, Chiyoda-ku, tel: 3593-7322.* Heichinrou serves contemporary Cantonese cuisine at its most flavourful, prepared by Hong Kong chefs and featuring plenty of fresh seafood. You get great views over the city, too. Located just outside Tameike-sanno station.

Jap Cho Ok ¥¥ *Alteka Belte Plaza B1F, 4-1-15 Minami-Aoyama, Minato-ku, tel: 5410-3408.* This was the first Korean restaurant in Tokyo to serve multi-course vegetarian meals (as well as more standard Korean barbecues). The striking decor mixes modern and traditional motifs. Located on Gaeien-nishi-dori near Gaeienmae station.

Kozue ¥¥¥ *Park Hyatt Tokyo 40F, 3-7-1-2 Nishi-Shinjuku, Shinjuku-ku, tel: 5323-3460.* The place to go in Tokyo for a full-course, star-quality traditional Japanese meal, with the kind of extras you wouldn't get at a Shitamachi *ryotei* – like menus in English and table seating instead of *tatami* mats. Kozue is very pricey, but the food is exquisite. There's a great selection of rare premium sake and a breathtaking view of the city. Open daily for lunch and dinner. Reservations recommended.

Maisen ¥¥ *4-8-5 Jingumae, Shibuya-ku, tel: 3470-0071.* This chain specialises in *tonkatsu* (pork cutlets), but also offers shrimp and fried oyster options. The novelty here at the main branch is the setting: in a converted bathhouse just off the main Omotesando strip. Telltale signs of its origins are the high ceilings and the two carp ponds.

Nakase ¥¥¥-¥¥¥¥ *1-39-13 Akasaka, Taito-ku, tel: 3841-4015.* Delicious tempura served in a small traditional restaurant, near Senso-ji temple. Ask for *tatami*-mat seating by the lovely interior garden (especially in May, when the wisteria is in bloom) but expect to pay more for it. Open lunch and dinner, closed Tuesday. No credit cards.

Ninja ¥¥ *Akasaka Tokyu Plaza 1F, 2-14-3 Nagatacho, Chiyoda-ku, tel: 5157-3936, www.ninjaakasaka.com.* Enter the portals of this theme restaurant and you're transported to a castle in ancient Japan, where you are served by ninja assassins in traditional black dress. The food is Japanese mixed with lots of Western and Asian flavours. Lots of fun for all the family. Reservations recommended.

Torafuku ¥¥–¥¥¥ *Aoyama Hanamo Bldg B1F, 3-12-9 Kita-Aoyama, Minato-ku, tel: 5766-2800.* The lunch scene at this classy yet inexpensive Japanese restaurant is always bustling, with *teishoku* set menus fuelling local office workers and designer types from nearby Omotesando. At night, *sashimi*, grilled fish and vegetable dishes are paired with top-shelf Niigata rice and sake. Communal seating encourages conviviality. Torafuku has a prime location at the intersection of Aoyama-dori and Kotto-dori.

Tsunahachi ¥ *3-31-8 Shinjuku, Shinjuku-ku, tel: 3352-1012, www.tunahachi.co.jp.* Tempura doesn't have to be expensive. Tsunahachi is a relic of earlier times, and so are its prices. Who cares if the smell of cooking oil permeates the building? This is how the locals eat.

Two Rooms ¥¥¥ *AO Bldg 5F, 3-11-7 Kita-Aoyama, Minato-ku, tel: 3498-0002, www.tworooms.jp.* This restaurant-lounge is run by a foreign management group that enjoys a stellar reputation among Tokyo foodies – and it shows. Both the high-end grill and the stand-alone bar have become mainstays of the local nightlife scene, with the al fresco lounge particularly busy in clement weather.

YAMANOTE (ROPPONGI)

Cicada ¥¥¥ *5-2-40 Minami-Azabu, Minato-ku, tel: 5447-5522.* Stylish but casual, Cicada serves excellent modern pan-Mediterranean cuisine, focusing especially on the foods of Spain and Morocco. It's highly popular with Tokyo's expats, so reservations are a must.

Fukuzushi ¥¥¥ *5-7-8 Roppongi, Minato-ku, tel: 3402-4116, www.roppongifukuzushi.com.* The elegant Fukuzushi is an ocean of calm away from the hubbub of Roppongi – even though it's just a block from the Tokyo branch of the Hard Rock Café. Not only is the sushi brilliant, Fukuzushi feels far less exclusive than many old-school Tokyo sushi shops.

Gonpachi ¥¥ *1-13-11 Nishi-Azabu, Minato-ku, tel: 5771-0170, www.gonpachi.jp.* The faux-traditional architecture makes it feel like a theme park, but the food – simple country-style *yakitori*, grilled pork or *soba* noodles – is surprisingly good. The third-floor sushi restaurant is more sophisticated.

Hainan Jeefan Shokudo ¥¥ *6-11-16 Roppongi, Minato-ku, tel: 5474-3200.* This cheerful little diner on a side street behind Roppongi Hills knocks out Singapore specialities, including lunch specials of Hainan-style chicken rice, and a large range of curries, stir-fries and spicy *laksa lemak* noodles in the evening. They have a small terrace that's very popular in summer.

Inakaya ¥¥¥–¥¥¥¥ *5-3-4 Roppongi, Minato-ku, tel: 3408-5040.* Part restaurant, part circus. You sit at a large U-shaped counter with an array of vegetables, seafood, beef and chicken in front of you. Tell the two cooks on the platform what you want, and they prepare it on the charcoal grill and hand it over on long wooden paddles – with lots of shouting and showmanship to speed things along. Located one block from Roppongi crossing.

L'Atelier de Joel Robuchon ¥¥¥¥ *Roppongi Hills Hillside 2F, 6-10-1 Roppongi, Minato-ku, tel: 5772-7500.* French chef Joel Robuchon's Tokyo 'atelier' is every bit as good as its counterpart in Paris. Sit at the counter, looking in at the open kitchen, and nibble on his tapas-inspired creations. You have to make a reservation for the 6pm sittings.

Mario i Sentieri ¥¥¥ *4-1-10 Nishi-Azabu, Minato-ku, tel: 6418-7072, http://mario-frittoli.com.* Mario Frittoli – a celebrity chef who attracts both Japanese and expat admirers – serves the cuisine of his native Tuscany with a modern twist and an emphasis on seasonal Japanese ingredients. His small, well-appointed dining room is also the scene of regular events ranging from wine dinners to musical performances. A classy place for a special meal.

Oak Door ¥¥¥ *Grand Hyatt Hotel 6F, 6-10-3 Roppongi, Minato-ku, tel: 4333-8888.* Match premium *wagyu* steaks, grilled in wood-fired open ovens, with high-octane New World wines from the gleaming, glass-enclosed cellar at this restaurant. This is expense-account territory, but immensely satisfying.

Rice Terrace ¥¥ *2-7-9 Nishi-Azabu, Minato-ku, tel: 3498-6271.* Secluded, intimate and sophisticated, Rice Terrace serves some of the best Thai food in Tokyo. The cuisine remains faithful to the original, but the spices are applied with subtlety, in deference to local palates. Just a five-minute walk towards Aoyama from Nishi-Azabu crossing.

YAMANOTE (SHIBUYA)

Beacon ¥¥¥ *1-2-5 Shibuya, Shibuya-ku, tel: 6418-0077.* This is a plush grill in the finest New York tradition. The steaks are first-rate, but there's also a good selection of seafood, and they serve brilliant burgers at lunchtime.

Kaikaya ¥¥ *23-7 Maruyamacho, Shibuya-ku, tel: 3770-0878.* Some *izakaya* (sake bars) can be standoffish if you're not a regular, but no such problem at Kaikaya. Casual and friendly, this is the perfect place to relax with some sake or beer, and then explore the wide range of seafood. Located near the west exit of Shinsen station on the Keio-Inokashira line.

Kanetanaka-so ¥¥¥ *Cerulean Tower Tokyu Hotel 2F, 26-1 Sakur-agaoka-cho, Shibuya-ku, tel: 3476-3420.* Japan's elevated *kaiseki* cuisine is reinterpreted in contemporary form here, harmonising Western influences with traditional recipes, in a Western setting with tables instead of *tatami*. There are no windows, but the multi-course meals are a picture in themselves.

Ninnikuya ¥¥¥ *1-26-12 Ebisu, Shibuya-ku, tel: 3446-5887.* New Age fusion-style cuisine with one special feature: the theme of every entrée is garlic. The recipes that owner-chef Endo Eiyuki has collected from around the world draw long queues to this little backstreet restaurant; you might have to share a table. Try the Peruvian garlic chicken. Open for dinner only, closed Sunday. No credit cards.

Tableaux ¥¥¥ *Sunroser Daikanyama Bldg B1, 11-6 Sarugaku-cho, Shibuya-ku, tel: 5489-2201.* Continental and California cuisines served up by Tokyo's most professional Western restaurateurs. The kind of place where the waiters know how every dish is made, and where if you come back a month later, the maître'd will remember your name. Located across from the popular Daikanyama Address shopping centre, Tableaux is open daily for lunch and dinner. Reservations recommended.

TSUKIJI/ODAIBA

Edo-Gin ¥¥¥ *4-5-1 Tsukiji, Chuo-ku, tel: 3543-4401.* Its location – a few minutes from the Central Wholesale Fish Market – and its venerable reputation ensure the best and freshest ingredients at this sushi bar. The generous portions of raw fish drape over and almost obscure the rice underneath. Sit at the counter and watch the chef at work. Open for lunch and dinner, closed Sunday.

Hapuna ¥¥¥ *Shinagawa Prince Hotel, 4-10-30 Takanawa, Minato-ku, tel: 5421-1114.* An elegant yet family friendly buffet restaurant, Hapuna is the perfect place to dine if you want to try a little of everything. The spread includes an amazing array of dishes from Japanese, Chinese and Western cuisine; the dessert buffet alone is worth the price of admission.

Sushi-Bun ¥¥ *Chuo Shijo Bldg No. 8, 5-2-1 Tsukiji, Chuo-ku, tel: 3541-3860.* Join the Tsukiji fish market workers for some of the freshest (and cheapest) sushi you've ever had. Just ask for the top-of-the-line *omakase* tasting menu. It's only a hole in the wall, so there are always queues. Opens early for the workers to eat, and closes at noon.

T.Y. Harbor Brewing Co. ¥¥ *Bond Street, 2-1-3 Higashi-Shinagawa, Shinagawa-ku, tel: 5479-4555.* This brewpub on the bay combines a vast selection of designer beers, porters and ales with a first-rate menu of Californian cuisine. The main dining room is vast; in good weather, the best seats in the house are on the terrace. Open daily for lunch and dinner. Reservations recommended.

A–Z TRAVEL TIPS

A Summary of Practical Information

A

ACCOMMODATION

Tokyo, alas, is not a city for 'charming' lodgings. Accommodation is clean, safe and reasonably efficient, but don't expect your hotel to be one of the fond memories of your visit. Nor are you likely to find a bargain: rates – wherever the location – are high.

Ordinarily, the further you stay from major attractions, the less it ought to cost you, but that rule doesn't really apply here. On the up-side, staying off the beaten path shouldn't pose any serious problems either. Few hotels are very far from a train or subway station.

No official organisation classifies or rates the hotels in Tokyo. In general, however, the accommodation you will want to consider falls into three categories: international hotels, business hotels and *ryokan* (Japanese-style inns).

International hotels are exactly what you would expect – pricey. The guest rooms are Western-style and Western-sized, with the usual extras: room service, toiletries in the bathroom, cable TV. There may be some Japanese-style rooms available (with *tatami* mats and futon beds), but these are more expensive. Usually there will be a business centre and a fitness club. Front desk staff will speak English.

Business hotels offer little more than a roof over your head. The rooms are small; singles can be downright claustrophobic. Amenities are minimal: a phone, a television, a pair of slippers and a robe. (You buy toiletries, if you need them, from a vending machine in the hall.) The bathrooms are prefabricated plastic units with low ceilings. There might be a restaurant and a night receptionist, but no room service or porter.

There are two kinds of *ryokan*. The more elegant ones are still typical of cities like Kyoto, but they have all but disappeared from Tokyo. The other type is a kind of low-budget pension, also with *tatami* rooms; not all of the rooms will have private baths. If you elect to have breakfast and dinner in, the meals will usually be served in a common dining room. There are a number of these in Tokyo, most of which are in the more traditional areas of the city. A list is available through the Japan National Tourist Organisation (see page 130).

> I'd like a single/double room **shinguru/daburu ruumu o on-egai shimas(u)**
> I'd like a room with shower/bath **basu/shawa tsuki no heya o onegai shimas(u)**
> May I see the room, please? **heya o misete kudasai?**

AIRPORTS

Tokyo is served by two airports. The majority of international flights arrive at **Narita International Airport** (NRT, www.narita-airport.jp), about 80km (50 miles) northeast of the city. The other airport, **Haneda** (HND, www.haneda-airport.jp), is used by most domestic flights, but a newly built international terminal has seen more overseas traffic head its way. Haneda is some 16km (10 miles) to the southwest.

To and from Narita. The Airport Limousine Bus and the Airport Express Bus run from Narita to major hotels in the city, to the JR Tokyo and Shinjuku stations, and to the Tokyo City Air Terminal. You can easily transfer to subways, trains or taxis from the latter destinations.

Tickets are for specific buses, and departure times are printed on them. They can be purchased in the arrivals lobby in both terminals, at counters facing the customs-clearance exits. The trip normally takes about an hour-and-a-half and is, generally speaking, the most economical way to get into the city.

JR Narita Express trains depart frequently from stations under both airport terminals, from 7.31am to 9.44pm, stopping at Tokyo station (journey time is just over an hour) and continuing on to Shinagawa, Shinjuku, Ikebukuro, Omiya or Yokohama. All seats are reserved; ticket prices are slightly higher than the bus, but the trains are not subject to traffic delays. There are also trains (on the Keisei line) that connect Narita to Ueno; these operate daily between 8.17am and 10.29pm. Keisei tickets are relatively inexpensive, but this option is to be recommended only if your destination is somewhere in the Ueno area.

Passengers leaving from Narita must pay a departure tax of ¥2,040 (there is no tax for children under two or for passengers in transit), although departure tax is now often included in the cost of the ticket.

To and from Haneda. The fastest and cheapest way from Haneda to the city is by monorail. Trains depart on the 20-minute ride to Tokyo's Hamamatsu-cho station every five minutes or so, from 5.11am to 12.05am. There are also direct trains on the Keikyu line to and from Shinagawa.

Taxis. Taxis from Narita to central Tokyo will cost ¥20,000 and upwards, depending on your destination; from Haneda, the cost will be approximately ¥8,000.

B

BUDGETING FOR YOUR TRIP

Air travel. As with any holiday destination, airfares to Tokyo will vary considerably with the time of year. If you're flying in the off-season, you should be able to get a discounted return ticket to Tokyo from London for under £700.

Airport transfer and tax. About ¥8,000 per person.

Accommodation. A comfortable double room with private bath in any reasonably convenient location will cost at least ¥12,000 and can easily be twice that.

Meals. A light 'breakfast set' at a coffee shop will cost around ¥650; lunch deals have become very competitive, with set meals around ¥1,000, even in popular sightseeing areas like Ginza. Dinner is a more daunting prospect: expect to pay upwards of ¥3,000 for a decent meal and as much as ¥8,000 for something truly memorable.

Public transport. Getting around the city should cost you no more than ¥1,000 a day. The base taxi fare is around ¥700; most destinations within central Tokyo are reachable for under ¥3,000.

Miscellaneous. For museum admissions and other incidentals, budget another ¥2,000 per day.

C

CAR HIRE

Tokyo has one of the world's most efficient mass-transit systems, so there's little need to drive. If you're exploring further afield (Nikko, for example, or the Japan Alps) and you really must drive, there are car-hire agency outlets within hailing distance of every prefectural city railway station. Book ahead in Tokyo, pick up the car at your destination, and drop it off on your way back. Be aware that often no English is spoken at either the Tokyo reservation centres or local agencies. There are no age restrictions, but you will need a credit card and an international licence; your home-country licence is not valid. Expect to pay about ¥12,000 for a mid-size vehicle, including mandatory insurance coverage.

Nippon Rent-a-Car: tel: 3485-7196, www.nipponrentacar.co.jp
Nissan Rent-a-Car: tel: 0120-00-4123 toll free, https://nissan-rentacar.com
Toyota Rent-a-Car: tel: 0800-700-0815 toll free, http://rent.toyota.co.jp

CLIMATE

For clear skies and comfortable temperatures, the best times to be in Tokyo are from mid-April to mid-June and during October. Even then, pack for the possibility of wet weather – Tokyo gets a lot of it.

The *tsuyu* (rainy season) lasts from mid-June until mid-July. August brings heat and unrelenting high humidity. The typhoons that form in the western Pacific in late summer and early autumn have usually lost most of their force by the time they get as far north as Tokyo, but can still cause torrential storms.

Winter in Tokyo is cold enough to require sweaters and overcoats, but seldom brings heavy snowfalls.

Average daily temperatures in Tokyo are as follows:

	J	F	M	A	M	J	J	A	S	O	N	D
Max °F	46	48	53	62	72	75	82	86	78	70	60	51
Min °F	29	30	35	46	53	62	70	72	66	56	42	33
Max °C	8	9	12	17	22	24	28	30	26	21	16	11
Min °C	-2	-1	2	8	12	17	21	22	19	13	6	1

CRIME AND SAFETY

Despite rising crime rates, Tokyo has a relatively low level of street crime. Some caution is necessary at street festivals, where pickpockets are occasionally at work, and women on crowded trains and subways might suffer unwelcome attention. But visitors have virtually nothing to fear – night or day – from muggings, rapes or armed robberies. Much-publicised acts of random street violence are on the increase, but foreign visitors are unlikely to be targeted.

In the unlikely event that you are the victim of a crime, report it immediately to the police (dial 110 from any phone) and to your embassy. The police switchboard will connect you to an English-speaking officer.

D

DRIVING (see Car Hire)

It is highly unlikely you will need to drive when in Tokyo; if you do, be aware that streets tend to be narrow, and parking is limited.

Driving in Japan is on the left. The speed limit on city streets is 40kmh (25mph). Petrol prices are somewhere between US and UK prices, but are subject to fluctuations. Petrol stations can be hard to find, and few of them stay open past 9pm or 10pm.

E

ELECTRICITY

The current in Tokyo is 100v/50Hz AC. Plugs have the same two flat prongs as those in the US. Hotel rooms do not usually have grounded outlets for three-pronged plugs, but they are sometimes available in hotel business centres. Multi-current travel appliances will work fine in Japan; for anything else, you might need an adapter. Hair dryers will not work in the 110-volt safety outlets (for shavers) in hotel bathrooms.

EMBASSIES AND CONSULATES

Australia 2-1-14 Mita, Minato-ku, tel: 5232-4111, www.australia.or.jp/en

Canada 7-3-38 Akasaka, Minato-ku, tel: 5412-6200, www.canada international.gc.ca/japan-japon

Ireland 2-10-7 Kojimachi, Chiyoda-ku, tel: 3263-0695, www.embassy ofireland.jp/en

New Zealand 20-40 Kamiyama-cho, Shibuya-ku, tel: 3467-2271, www.nzembassy.com/japan

South Africa 1-4 Kojimachi, Chiyoda-ku, tel: 3265-3366, www.sa japan.org

UK 1 Ichiban-cho, Chiyoda-ku, tel: 5211-1100, www.ukinjapan.fco.gov.uk/en

US 1-10-5 Akasaka, Minato-ku, tel: 3224-5000, http://japan.us embassy.gov

EMERGENCIES

For a police emergency, dial 110 from any phone. To call an ambulance or report a fire, dial 119.

Tokyo English Life Line (tel: 5774-0992) is an English-language distress hotline available daily 9pm–11pm. Volunteer counsellors will relay your emergency to the appropriate Japanese agency. Assistance in English is also available 24 hours a day on the Japan Helpline (tel: 0570-000-911, 0120-461-997 toll free).

Call the police! **keesatsu o yonde**
Find a doctor! **isha o yonde**
Help! **tas(u)kete**
I'm lost. **michi ni mayoi mash(i)ta.**

G

GAY AND LESBIAN TRAVELLERS

Japan is not particularly hostile to homosexuality, although it is not a life-choice asserted as openly as it is in some Western cultures. Visitors might find the gay and lesbian nightlife scene a little difficult to discover. The best-known quarter is Shinjuku Ni-chome, but there are clubs, discos and drag bars in Roppongi and other areas as well.

GETTING THERE

There are direct flights to Narita (and, increasingly, Haneda) from virtually every international hub in the world.
From Australia: Japan Airlines and Qantas.
From Canada: Air Canada, Canadian Airlines and Japan Airlines.
From Ireland: Aer Lingus.
From New Zealand: Air New Zealand and ANA.
From South Africa: Air France and South African Airways.
From the UK: All Nippon Airways, British Airways, Japan Airlines and Virgin Atlantic Airways.
From the US: All Nippon Airways, American Airlines, Delta, Japan Airlines, and United Airlines. The national carriers of Singapore, Thailand and Korea also fly to Tokyo from destinations in the US on onwards flights.

GUIDES AND TOURS

Organised tours. The most popular organised sightseeing tours of Tokyo are by bus. Hato Bus (tel: 3435-6081, www.hatobus.com), JTB/Sunrise Tours (tel: 5796-5454, www.japanican.com), and Japan Gray Line (www.jgl.co.jp) offer bus tours with English-speaking guides, including visits to the Imperial Palace East Garden, a tea ceremony, and/or a river cruise to the Senso-ji Temple in Asakusa. Tours are either half-day or full-day and include pick-up and return at major hotels. There are also evening tours, which include a kabuki performance, a geisha show or a cabaret floor show. The cost ranges from about ¥4,000 to ¥12,000 per person. Tokyo Shitamachi Bus (www.kotsu.metro.tokyo.jp) operates every 30 minutes between popular downtown areas such as Ueno and Asakusa; fares are just ¥200 per ride.

Walking tours. Tours for groups of up to five people, mostly on foot, can be arranged through Tokyo Tourism Volunteers. Fees range from free to about ¥3,000. Details at www.gotokyo.org (under Recommended Courses).

Private tour guides. The Japan Guide Association (tel: 3213-2706) can put you in touch with an accredited English-speaking guide for a personalised tour. You can then negotiate the fee and itinerary with the guide. Fees will depend on where you want to go, and for how long: about ¥20,000–30,000 for a full day.

H

HEALTH AND MEDICAL CARE

Ensure you have a comprehensive travel insurance package recognised in Japan for outpatient treatment and hospitalisation. If you have a particular medical condition that might cause a problem on your trip, contact your embassy as soon as possible when you arrive in Tokyo. The consular section maintains a list of English-speaking doctors, with information on their specialisation, where they trained, their office hours and which insurance plans they accept.

International hotels often have an arrangement with a doctor or clinic for referrals in case of sudden minor illness. If you need to go to a hospital, remember that first-time consultations are usually scheduled for morning hours.

Hospitals

Tokyo Midtown Medical Centre: Midtown Tower 6F, 9-7-1 Akasaka, Minato-ku, tel: 5413-0080; http://tokyomidtown-mc.jp

St Luke's International Hospital: 9-1 Akashi-cho, Chuo-ku, tel: 3541-5151; www.luke.or.jp

Seibo International Catholic Hospital: 2-5-1 Naka-Ochiai, Shinjuku-ku, tel: 3951-1111

Tokyo Medical and Surgical Clinic: Mori Building 32, 2F, 3-4-30 Shiba Koen, Minato-ku, tel: 3436-3028; www.tmsc.jp

Pharmacies. There are no 24-hour pharmacies in Tokyo. Convenience stores carry a few basic non-prescription medicines. The American Pharmacy (Marunouchi Building, Floor B1, 1-1-1 Marunouchi, Chiyoda-ku, tel: 5220-7716; Mon–Fri 9am–9pm, Sat 10am–9pm and Sun 10am–8pm) carries a range of American and European medications.

L

LANGUAGE

Japanese is highly unusual in that it is part of no larger language group. However, its written form bears some similarity with Chinese, as the Japanese adopted Chinese ideograms for their writing.

Japanese is composed less of vowels and consonants than of syllables, consisting of a consonant and a vowel. All syllables are pronounced with equal force – there is no stress – except for emphasis.

good morning **ohayoo gozaimasu**
hello/good afternoon **kon-nichi-wa**
good evening **konban-wa**

good night **oyasumi nasai**
goodbye **sayonara**
please (asking for a favour) **onegai shimasu**
thank you **arigatoo**
yes/no **hai/iie**
excuse me **sumimasen**
I don't understand **wakarimasen**
How much? **ikura des(u) ka**

M

MAPS AND STREET NAMES

The best district-by-district street guide is *Tokyo: A Bilingual Atlas*, published by Kodansha International, which also has subway and railway maps; place-names are printed in both English and Japanese. The Japan National Tourist Organisation provides free maps of the city, available at the Tourist Information Centre (see page 130). Hotel kiosks and bookstores also have a wide variety of pocket maps,

Postal addresses in Tokyo are notoriously hard to fathom. In the vernacular they are written in descending order of priority: prefecture, city, ward, block, sub-block and building name. This order is reversed when written in Roman letters (the order used in this guide). Central Tokyo is divided into 23 wards (known as *ku*), each of which contains numerous districts (*cho*), each with its own name, which are subdivided into smaller units (*banchi*) and then smaller units (*go*), which are usually individual buildings. Thus, to track down 1-2-3 Marunouchi, Chiyoda-ku, you would look for Chiyoda Ward on the map, then look for the Marunouchi district, then the 1st *cho*, the 2nd *banchi* and finally the 3rd *go*. However, there is often little logic to the sequence and layout. Finding a destination from an address requires a detailed city map and then much legwork and asking directions. First try the local police boxes (*koban*), small police substations that oversee their own small area. Taxi drivers rarely know precise locations from the address, apart from major landmarks and hotels.

MEDIA

The locally produced English-language newspapers are the *Japan Times* and the *Daily Yomiuri*. These are available in hotels and at most railway and subway kiosks. A few hotel bookshops also carry imported newspapers. The best source of information in English about the city's bars, restaurants, concerts and events is the free biweekly *Metropolis*, widely available and updated online each week.

Cable/satellite TV service in the international hotels includes CNN, BBC and several local English-language information channels. The Japanese commercial networks have occasional dual-language broadcasts of foreign films. NHK, Japan's public broadcaster, has two terrestrial television channels, plus two satellite channels and a radio network. The main terrestrial TV channel offers nightly bilingual news broadcasts.

The Armed Forces Far East Network (FEN) is an all-English news-and-music radio station that also carries syndicated programmes from the US. One of the more popular local radio stations for music and news in English is Inter FM.

MONEY

Yen notes are issued in denominations of ¥10,000, ¥5,000, ¥2,000 and ¥1,000; coins are ¥500, ¥100, ¥50, ¥10, ¥5 and ¥1. ¥5,000 and ¥10,000 notes can be comfortably used for even the smallest purchases.

Currency exchange. International hotels will change either travellers' cheques or foreign currency (if exchange quotations are available) into yen. Accredited banks will do the same – at slightly better rates. With the liberalisation of financial regulations, stores in many tourist areas are increasingly able to accept payment in currencies other than yen; you will need to present your passport.

ATMs and credit cards. The number of places where you can use an international credit card and PIN number to make spot cash withdrawals remains limited. Look for branches of Citibank and post offices. Providing you exercise a little caution, carrying cash on you is usually not a problem. For larger expenditures, Visa, American Express and MasterCard are widely accepted in restaurants and shops. Travellers' cheques are not.

Banks. Citibank (tel: 0120-50-4189 toll-free) offers assistance about financial matters in English. Branches in popular areas include Otemachi (1-1-3 Otemachi, Chiyoda-ku) and Omotesando (3-11-7 Kita-Aoyama, Minato-ku).

> I'd like to change some money **o-kane o kaetain des(u) ga**
> I'd like to change some travellers' cheques **toraberazu chekku o kankin sh(i)tain des(u)**
> Where are the cash machines? **kyasshu kona wa doko des(u) ka**

OPENING TIMES

Stores in the major shopping districts generally open at 10am and close at 7pm or 8pm. Business and government offices open at 9am and close to the public at 5pm, although workers might be at their desks far into the evening. Bank hours are 9am to 3pm.

Apart from Meiji-jingu, the precincts of Shinto shrines are open for worshippers and other visitors to enter at any time. Buddhist temples are normally open dawn until dusk, but those that charge entry usually open at 8.30 or 9am. Most museums are closed on Monday; however, if a national holiday falls on a Monday, then they usually stay open and close the following day.

Dining early is the norm in Tokyo; most restaurants take their last orders at 10pm or earlier (see page 100). The last screening at all but a few of the first-run cinemas is around 7pm. Concerts and theatre performances have similar schedules. However, in entertainment quarters like Shinjuku, Ikebukuro and Roppongi, bars stay open through the night.

P

POLICE (see Crime and Safety)

You can dial the police number (110) free from any public phone. Chances are you won't have to walk more than a few blocks to find one of the local police substations (*koban*) scattered strategically throughout the city. The officer on duty will be helpful and, if he can't speak English, will have recourse to someone who can.

> I've lost my... ...o nak(u)shi mash(i)ta
> wallet/handbag/passport saifu/handobaggu/pas(u)pooto

POST OFFICES

You can buy stamps and post letters and postcards at virtually any hotel. Most branch post-office counters are open Monday–Friday, but you can drop off mail or buy stamps from vending machines in the lobby on Saturdays. An airmail letter from Japan to Europe, North America or Oceania is ¥110 (for 25g/1 oz or less); the rate for a postcard to any place in the world is ¥70. The postal service is fast and reliable.

PUBLIC HOLIDAYS

There are national holidays throughout the year in Japan, but during the so-called 'Golden Week' (end of April/beginning of May) there are four holidays. Every method of transport (domestic and international) and all holiday accommodation is booked solid. The same is true during the unofficial holiday period known as *O-bon*, celebrated in mid-August. Plan your trip to avoid these periods.

On the following holidays, banks and offices will be closed, but stores and restaurants will likely be unaffected. The exception is the

New Year period (30 December to 3 January), when virtually everything shuts down. When a holiday falls on a Sunday, the Monday after is also observed as a holiday.

1 January New Year's Day (*Ganjitsu*)
2nd Mon January Coming-of-Age Day (*Seijin no hi*)
11 February National Foundation Day (*Kenkoku kinen no hi*)
21 March Spring Equinox (*Shunbun no hi*)
29 April Showa Day (*Showa no hi*)
3 May Constitution Day (*Kenpo Kinenbi*)
4 May Greenery Day (*Midori no hi*)
5 May Children's Day (*Kodomo no hi*)
20 July Ocean Day (*Umi no hi*)
15 September Respect for the Aged Day (*Keiro no hi*)
23 September Autumnal Equinox (*Shunbun no hi*)
2nd Mon October Health and Sports Day (*Taiku no hi*)
3 November Culture Day (*Bunka no hi*)
23 November Labour Thanksgiving Day (*Kinro kansha no hi*)
23 December Emperor's Birthday (*Tenno tanjo bi*)

T

TELEPHONES

When calling from abroad, the country code for Japan is 81 and the city code for Tokyo is 3. To call Tokyo from other places in Japan, you must dial 03. To make a direct overseas call from Japan, dial 001-010 before the country code. For an English-speaking international operator dial 0051. Some payphones, including phone boxes on the street, will have gold plates, indicating in English that they can be used for international calls. You can call any country from one of these, using prepaid debit cards (sold in hotels, convenience stores and vending machines) in denominations of ¥1,000–¥10,000.

Note that placing long-distance calls from your hotel room will usually result in extra fees and charges, sometimes undisclosed.

Four Japanese companies offer direct-dial service: the preface codes are 001 (for KDDI), 0033 (NTT Communications), 0041 (Japan Telecom) and 0061 (Cable & Wireless IDC).

Rental mobile phones. Rental mobile phones are available at many locations in Narita Airport. Of the three major mobile-phone companies (NTT DoCoMo, Au and Softbank), DoCoMo (tel: 0120-680-100, www.mobilerental.jp) and Softbank (tel: 3560-7730, www.softbank-rental.jp) provide rentals for use within Japan. Softbank's rental is ¥250–¥1,575 per day depending on the plan, with outgoing calls charged at ¥105 per minute (incoming calls are free). You need to show a passport and give a Japanese address, and you will be billed directly from a credit card. You can pick up the handsets at Narita Airport or at selected Softbank shops, or get them sent to your hotel.

Alternatively, you can buy a prepaid mobile phone with prepaid cards available for ¥3,000 or ¥5,000 (valid 60 days). Calls are charged at ¥90 per minute.

> Where's the nearest telephone? **ichiban chikai denwa wa doka des(u) ka**
> I'd like to buy a phonecard, please **terehon kado o kudasai**

TIME ZONE

Tokyo is nine hours ahead of GMT. Japan has no daylight-saving time. The following chart shows the time in various cities in winter:

San Francisco	New York	London	Cape Town	**Tokyo**	Sydney
7pm	10pm	3am	5am	**noon**	1pm

TIPPING

Tipping isn't practised anywhere. An exception might be at a *ryotei* (a traditional restaurant with private dining rooms), where one of the staff will wait on you exclusively. In such cases, it's customary to leave ¥1,000 or ¥2,000, depending on the size of your party.

TOILETS

There are public toilets in most of Tokyo's parks and in all railway and subway stations. They are free and usually clean. Most department stores and large office buildings have toilets on the ground floor or in the basement, and no one will object if you use them. Be aware that – except in very rare instances – public facilities will have toilet paper but no paper towels or electric hand dryers.

Where are the toilets? **toire wa doko des(u) ka?**
ladies/gents **jose/danse**

TOURIST INFORMATION

Before your trip. The Japan National Tourist Organisation (JNTO; www.jnto.go.jp) has a network of offices in several countries.

New York: 11 West 42nd Street, 19th Floor New York, NY 10036, tel: (212) 757-5640, www.japantravelinfo.com.

Los Angeles: 515 South Figueroa Street, Suite 1470, Los Angeles, CA 90071, tel: (213) 623-1952, www.japantravelinfo.com.

London: 5th Floor, 12/13 Nicholas Lane, London, EC4N 7BN, tel: (020) 7398-5670, www.seejapan.co.uk.

Singapore: 16 Raffles Quay, 15-09 Hong Leong Building, Singapore 048581, tel: 6223-8205, www.jnto.org.sg.

Sydney: Suite 1, Level 4, 56 Clarence Street, Sydney, NSW 2000, tel: 02-9279 2177, www.jnto.org.au.

Toronto: 481 University Avenue, Suite 306, Toronto, ON M5G 2E9, tel: (416) 366-7140, www.jnto.go.jp/canada.

After you arrive. The main JNTO Tourist Information Centre in Tokyo is on the 10th floor of the Kotsu Kaikan Building, 2-10-1 Yurakucho, Chiyoda-ku, tel: 3201-3331. The centre is open daily 9am–5pm.

It also operates the Welcome Inn Reservation Centre in the same location (open daily 9am–noon and 1–5pm, www.itcj.jp), assisting tourists to make reservations at budget hotels and inns throughout Japan.

> Where is the tourist office? **kanko an-nai-jo doko**
> Do you have information on…? **…no an-nai wa arimas(u) ka**
> Are there any trips to…? **…e no tsuaa wa arimas(u) ka**

TRANSPORT

Tokyo has an excellent public transport system. It is efficient, clean and safe, and will take you within convenient walking distance of virtually anywhere you'll want to go. Colour-coded and well marked, it's almost as easy for a foreign visitor to use (except for the bus network) as it is for local commuters.

Trains. Japan Railways' Yamanote line trains (silver with green stripes) make a 35km (22-mile) loop around the central wards of the city: a total of 29 stops in all, including the major hub stations of Tokyo, Shibuya, Shinjuku and Ueno. The JR Chuo line (orange) and Sobu line (yellow) bisect the loop from east to west through the loop from Tokyo to the distant suburb of Takao. Be aware that some trains do not stop at every station. The Keihin Tohoku line (blue) connects Saitama Prefecture, to the north of Tokyo, with Kanagawa Prefecture, to the south; for part of that journey, the tracks run parallel to the Yamanote line loop.

Yamanote line fares are ¥130–¥250 depending on the distance. You purchase your ticket (valid only for the date of purchase) at a vending machine, and it is swallowed by the automatic turnstile at your destination. Prepaid debit cards, known as Suica, can be bought (¥500) and topped up at any station office: at vending machines with orange panels, you insert the card, press the screen for a ticket to your destination, and the cost is deducted automatically. You can also use your Japan Rail Pass on all JR trains.

Yamanote and Sobu line trains operate from about 4.30am to

around 12.30 at night. Between 8am and 9.30am and between 6pm and 9pm, the trains are especially packed with commuters.

Subways. There are 13 subway lines in Tokyo; trains run around every five minutes from about 5am to midnight. There are English-language maps of the system in every station, and bilingual signs at entrances. Subway fares begin at ¥160. A new prepaid, recharge-able card system known as PASMO, similar to Suica, can be used on subways, JR trains and buses. Cards can also be used in some stores and vending machines that carry the PASMO mark, instead of cash. Cards can be bought in various denominations at station offices and vending machines, and topped up by bus drivers or at stations.

You can use the same ticket to transfer from one subway line to another. At some stations this is easy; at others, there are long underground passageways between transfer turnstiles. All stations have numbered exit signs that indicate the nearest buildings, streets or intersections. At most stations there are signs in English and lifts.

Buses. The Tokyo bus network is extremely complicated, and there are no maps available in English.

Taxis and hire cars. Tokyo taxi fares are reasonable: an initial charge of around ¥700 is made, and about ¥80 is charged for every quarter mile thereafter. A 30 percent surcharge is added between 11pm and 5am. Cabs are clean, and drivers are honest and usually courteous. If the cab already has a fare, there will be a green light on the dashboard; if it is available, the light is red. At night, especially after 11pm, cabs are at a premium in the major entertainment quarters.

Where can I get a taxi? **tak(u)shii wa doko de nore mas(u) ka?**
How much will the journey cost? **ikura ni narimas(u) ka**
How do I get back to the station? **eki niwa doo yatte ikemas(u) ka**
Where's the ticket office? **kippu uriba wa dokko des(u) ka**

single/return **katamichi/ofuku**

V

VISAS AND ENTRY REQUIREMENTS

You will need a passport to enter Japan. Tourist visas are not required for citizens of Australia, Canada, Ireland, New Zealand, the UK or the US. Citizens of countries that have no reciprocal waiver agreements with Japan will need a visa, normally valid for one arrival and departure within a 90-day period. Due to increased security concerns, all foreign visitors must now undergo a fingerprint scan.

Non-residents can bring in 400 cigarettes or 100 cigars or 500 grams of tobacco, three bottles of spirits and 2 ounces of perfume. The importation of firearms, pornography and narcotics is strictly forbidden. There is no limit to the amount of money in your home currency you can bring in, nor any minimum per diem amount that must be converted to yen. On departure, you must inform customs if you intend to take out more than ¥1 million in Japanese currency.

Y

YOUTH HOSTELS

Asakusa Ryokan Toukaiso: 2-16-12 Nishi-Asakusa Taito-ku, tel: 3844-5618, www.toukaisou.com; ¥2,600

K's House Tokyo: 3-20-10 Kuramae, Taito-ku, tel: 5833-0444, http://kshouse.jp/tokyo-e/index.html; ¥2,800

Sakura Hostel Tokyo: 2-24-2 Asakusa, Taito-ku, tel: 3847-8111, www.sakura-hostel.co.jp; ¥2,940

Tokyo Central Youth Hostel: 18F, 1-1 Kaguragashi, Shinjuku-ku, tel: 3235-1107, www.jyh.gr.jp/tcyh; ¥3,960.

YMCA Asia Youth Centre: 2-5-5 Sarugaku-cho, Chiyoda-ku, tel: 3233-0611, http://ymcajapan.org/ayc/hotel/en/index.html.

Recommended Hotels

Although character is sometimes in short supply, there are very few sub-standard lodgings in Tokyo. Almost any hotel you choose will be clean, efficient and reasonably close to some form of public transport. Most staff will speak at least passable English, but only in the more expensive hotels will you find rooms with the space and amenities you would expect from hotels at home.

Recommendations are in four price categories, based on the daily cost of a minimum-rate double room, excluding service charges and taxes. A 5 percent consumer tax is added to all hotel bills. Another 5 percent local tax is added to final bills exceeding ¥15,000. At some hotels, a service charge of 10–15 percent is also added to the total bill.

¥¥¥¥	over ¥30,000
¥¥¥	¥20,000–30,000
¥¥	¥10,000–20,000
¥	below ¥10,000

MARUNOUCHI/GINZA/HIBIYA/SHINBASHI

Conrad Tokyo ¥¥¥¥ *Tokyo Shiodome Bldg, 1-9-1 Higashi-Shinbashi, Minato-ku, tel: 6388-8000, www.conradtokyo.co.jp.* Plush, spacious, tranquil, the Conrad occupies the top 10 floors of a 37-storey high-rise in Shiodome, with large guest rooms overlooking the Rainbow Bridge and the Tokyo waterfront. Its four restaurants include British chef Gordon Ramsay's first venture in the Far East. There's a 25m (80ft) swimming pool. 290 rooms.

Four Seasons Hotel Tokyo at Marunouchi ¥¥¥¥ *Pacific Century Place, 1-11-1 Marunouchi, Chiyoda-ku, tel: 5222-7222, www.fourseasons. com/marunouchi.* Spacious guest rooms, luxurious interiors, seamless service: this is what you expect at the Four Seasons. What makes the Marunouchi different is the intimate scale, the sleek, contemporary decor and high-tech amenities, as well as the unobtrusive location in a glass-clad tower overlooking Tokyo station and Tokyo International Forum. 57 rooms.

Hotel Villa Fontaine Shiodome ¥¥ *1-9-2 Higashi-Shinbashi, Minato-ku, tel: 3569-2220, www.hvf.jp.* The Villa Fontaine group has made its reputation through efficient service, contemporary decor and competitive value. Here they bring this winning formula to the upmarket Shiodome complex. Singles, though small, start from just ¥13,000, representing brilliant value for those on a limited budget. 497 rooms.

Imperial Hotel ¥¥¥ *1-1-1 Uchisaiwai-cho, Chiyoda-ku, tel: 3504-1111, www.imperialhotel.co.jp.* Tokyo lost something precious when Frank Lloyd Wright's brilliant 1922 Imperial Hotel was torn down in 1967 and replaced with this high-rise version. Still, the accommodation is spacious, the service is spot-on, and the location is ideal for excursions to the Imperial Palace and Ginza. Wheelchair access. 931 rooms.

Palace Hotel ¥¥¥ *1-1-1 Marunouchi, Chiyoda-ku, tel: 3211-5211, www.palacehoteltokyo.com.* Reopened in 2012 following a massive three-year renovation, the Palace Hotel now has an ambience to match its prime location across the street from the Imperial Palace. The spacious 290 rooms include smart details like Imabari bed linens and complimentary Maruyama Nori teas. The service remains gracious and smooth, and there is wheelchair access.

Peninsula Tokyo ¥¥¥ *1-8-1 Yurakucho, Chiyoda-ku, tel: 6270-2888, www.peninsula.com/tokyo.* This stand-alone property from the celebrated Peninsula group is notable for its huge suites and top-end restaurants. The hotel anchors one end of the revitalised Marunouchi business and shopping district, and the lobby lounge is popular with ladies who lunch. 314 rooms.

Ryumeikan Tokyo ¥¥ *1-3-22 Yaesu, Chuo-ku, tel: 3271-0971, http://ryumeikan-tokyo.jp.* Close to the Yaesu exit of Tokyo station, this hotel is difficult to beat for location. The rooms throughout are designed in Japanese-style. So, too, is the breakfast, typically consisting of fish, rice, miso soup and pickles, a good introduction to the way most Japanese used to start their day (breakfast is included in the price).

NIHOMBASHI/ASAKUSA/KANDA

Asakusa View Hotel ¥¥¥ *3-17-1 Nishi-Asakusa, Taito-ku, tel: 3847-1111, www.viewhotels.co.jp/asakusa.* The only modern hotel with pretensions to Western-style luxury in the Senso-ji temple area, the 337-room Asakusa View also has communal cypress-wood baths overlooking a sixth-floor Japanese garden.

Hilltop (Yama-no-ue) Hotel ¥¥ *1-1 Kanda-Surugadai, Chiyoda-ku, tel: 3293-2311, www.yamanoue-hotel.co.jp.* The low-rise, 74-room Hilltop is one of the only Tokyo hotels that can boast history, patina and atmosphere, and it has long been a retreat for local writers and intellectuals.

Mandarin Oriental ¥¥¥ *2-1-1 Nihonbashi-Muromachi, Chuo-ku, tel: 3270-8800, www.mandarinoriental.com/tokyo.* Occupying the top eight floors of the 38-storey Mitsui Tower, it gives spectacular views in all directions from its 179 plush guest rooms and starred restaurants. Lies in the historic Nihonbashi district, close to the Stock Exchange.

Royal Park Hotel ¥¥¥ *2-1-1 Nihonbashi Kakigara-cho, Chuo-ku, tel: 3667-1111, www.rph.co.jp.* The big, comfortable lobby is a good indication of the size of the accommodation upstairs. South-facing rooms on the sixth to eighth floors overlook a charming Japanese garden. One special boon is the hotel corridor right into Tokyo City Air Terminal, where you can check your baggage through to your destination and hop on a bus for Narita Airport. Wheelchair access.

Sakura Ryokan ¥ *2-6-2 Iriya, Taito-ku, tel: 3876-8118, www.sakura-ryokan.com.* This welcoming, family-run *ryokan* in the old quarter of Iriya has a mix of comfortable Japanese- and Western-style rooms. Specify if you want a room with bath, otherwise guests share the communal bathrooms on each floor. An interesting ten-minute walk from the temples and shrines of Asakusa.

AKASAKA/TORANOMON/ROPPONGI

Akasaka Yoko Hotel ¥¥ *6-14-12 Akasaka, Minato-ku, tel: 3586-4050, www.yokohotel.co.jp.* Equidistant between Roppongi and Akasaka, this is an affordable business-hotel option in an otherwise expensive uptown area of the city. The staff are friendly and speak English. The rooms are a little on the small side, but clean and well equipped.

Capitol Hotel Tokyu ¥¥¥¥ *2-10-3 Nagata-cho, Chiyoda-ku, tel: 3503-0109, www.capitolhoteltokyu.com*. Designed by renowned architect Kengo Kuma, this flagship property of the leading Tokyu hotels group opened in 2010. The 251 spacious, Western-style rooms feature cool Japanese design touches and floor-to-ceiling windows, and the location is just a walk away from many top sightseeing spots.

Grand Hyatt Tokyo ¥¥¥¥ *6-10-3 Roppongi, Minato-ku, tel: 4333-1234, www.tokyo.grandhyatt.com*. Thanks to its luxurious amenities and location inside the Roppongi Hills complex, the Grand Hyatt has rapidly become a favourite of visiting VIPs, as well as the city's expat community. Its restaurants include the Oak Door grill, the exquisite Roku Roku sushi bar, and the stylish, modern French Kitchen; 389 rooms.

Hotel Ibis ¥¥ *7-14-4 Roppongi, Minato-ku, tel: 3403-4411, www.ibis-hotel.com*. An old favourite, located in the happening Roppongi area, near to excellent nightspots. Its facilities, which include clean, well-serviced rooms, Japanese, Vietnamese and Italian restaurants, and even a karaoke lounge, are good value.

Hotel New Otani ¥¥¥¥ *4-1 Kioi-cho, Chiyoda-ku, tel: 3265-1111, www.newotani.co.jp*. Along with the Imperial and the Okura, the New Otani is considered by locals to be one of Tokyo's 'big three' hotels. It's easy to see why – the sprawling grounds, roomy accommodation and world-class restaurants are complemented by impeccable Japanese hospitality.

Hotel Okura Tokyo ¥¥¥¥ *2-10-4 Toranomon, Minato-ku, tel: 3582-0111, www.hotelokura.co.jp/tokyo*. There are lots of reasons why the Okura is consistently rated by business travellers as being among the best two or three hotels in Asia: highlights include the tasteful muted ambience, the 858 spacious rooms and the impeccable service.

Ritz-Carlton Tokyo ¥¥¥ *9-7-1 Akasaka, Minato-ku, tel: 3423-8000, www.ritzcarlton.com.* Occupying eight floors atop Roppongi's tallest building, the Ritz-Carlton offers the same legendary service as its overseas counterparts – at the same sky-high rates. The spa and lobby lounge are considered among the best in the city, and the hotel's four exquisite Japanese restaurants offer a wide range of local dishes.

EBISU/SHIBUYA/SHINJUKU

Cerulean Tower Tokyo Hotel ¥¥¥ *26-1 Sakuragaoka-cho, Shibuya-ku, tel: 3476-3000, www.ceruleantower-hotel.com.* Dominating the skyline in Shibuya, the Cerulean Tower is the flagship of the Tokyu hotel chain. The 411 rooms are spacious though without great character. But you can't beat that view (including glimpses of Mt Fuji to the west), either from the guest rooms or the 40th-floor restaurants and bar.

Hilton Tokyo ¥¥¥ *6-6-2 Nishi-Shinjuku, Shinjuku-ku, tel: 3344-5111, www.hilton.com.* The lobby is undistinguished, but the rooms are comfortable and well appointed, with *shoji* sliding paper screens (instead of curtains) to let in and soften the light. Offers fine dining in French restaurant Le Pergolese, is within walking distance of the Tokyo Metropolitan Government buildings, and has wheelchair access. 801 rooms.

Hotel Mets Shibuya ¥¥ *3-29-17 Shibuya, Shibuya-ku, tel: 3409-0011, www.jrhotelgroup.com.* A welcoming business hotel run by the JR railway group, Mets offers a straightforward, inexpensive stay adjacent to Shibuya Station. Breakfast at the on-site coffee shop includes Japanese, Chinese and Western dishes. Some English spoken.

Park Hyatt Tokyo ¥¥¥ *3-7-1-2 Nishi-Shinjuku, Shinjuku-ku, tel: 5322-1234, http://tokyo.park.hyatt.com.* This hotel, the setting for the film *Lost in Translation*, occupies the 47th to 54th floors of a skyscraper. The 178 sumptuously appointed rooms – and even the bathrooms – have spectacular views of the Shinjuku skyline. Ultra-professional concierge service, remarkable restaurants, excellent health club, and wheelchair access.

Shibuya City Hotel ¥¥ *1-1 Maruyamacho, Shibuya-ku, tel: 5489-1010, www.shibuya-city-hotel.com.* Close to the 'love hotels', live-music clubs, and Bunkamura culture complex, you are in the thick of Shibuya life here, but in a boutique hotel that feels cosy, comfortable and friendly. Nicely decorated rooms and a helpful staff. Given the location, the rates are stunning. Just seven minutes' walk from Shibuya station.

Westin Tokyo ¥¥¥ *1-4-1 Mita, Meguro-ku, tel: 5423-7000, www.westin-tokyo.co.jp.* This hotel is the centrepiece of the Ebisu Garden Place development, a complex of high-rise apartments, shops, restaurants and cultural facilities. The no-expense-spared Art Nouveau lobby is fun, and the guest rooms are spacious. Wheelchair access.

MEJIRO

Four Seasons Hotel Tokyo at Chinzan-so ¥¥¥¥ *2-10-8 Sekiguchi, Bunkyo-ku, tel: 3943-2222, www.fourseasons.com/tokyo.* The location of this hotel, half an hour from any of the main tourist areas, is unfortunate. It boasts, however, one of the most beautiful settings in Tokyo (formerly the gardens of an imperial estate) and a tasteful and elegant ambience to match. Standard rooms are spacious; Conservatory Suites have private greenhouse patios. Wheelchair access.

SHINAGAWA/SHIROGANEDAI

Sheraton Miyako Hotel Tokyo ¥¥¥ *1-1-50 Shiroganedai, Minato-ku, tel: 3447-3111, www.miyakohotels.ne.jp.* Shiroganedai is one of Tokyo's most exclusive areas, with plenty of trees and open spaces and far from the inner city frenzy. This efficient, mid-sized hotel is comfortable and calm, with restaurants and lounges overlooking a lush garden.

Shinagawa Prince Hotel ¥¥ *4-10-30 Takanawa, Minato-ku, tel: 3440-1111, www.princehotels.com.* A favourite of business travellers and families, the expansive Shinagawa Prince Hotel offers a pool, cinema and even a bowling alley. But the most attractive feature is its proximity to Shinagawa station, which allows easy access to all areas of Tokyo and bullet train service for travels beyond.

INDEX

Berlitz pocket guide
Tokyo
Fourth Edition 2013

Written by Jared Lubarsky
Updated by Steve Trautlein
Edited by Catherine Dreghorn
Picture Researcher: Lucy Johnston
Series Editor: Tom Stainer
Production: Tynan Dean, Linton Donaldson and Rebeka Ellam

Photography credits: Akira Okada/JNTO 81; CORBIS 3BL, 17, 68, 82; Chris Stowers/Apa Publications 2TL, 3TR, 4B, 5T, 4/5B, 13, 14, 29, 38, 39, 43, 44, 45, 48, 49, 52, 54, 55, 56, 59, 62, 65, 69, 71, 72, 73, 77, 78, 79, 80, 85, 91, 98, 100, 102; JNTO 75; Mary Evans Picture Library 19; Ming Tang-Evans/Apa Publications 2BR, 2TR, 3TL, 4T, 4BC&R, 8, 10, 24, 26, 28, 35, 41, 46, 60, 66, 76, 87, 89, 93, 95, 104; Paolo Gianti/dreamstime 2BL; Q.Sawami/JNTO 1; Tokyo National Museum 16; Topfoto 21, 23; iStockphoto 32; Yasufumi Nishi/JNTO 50, 57, 67; Yuryz/Dreamstime.com 36; Andrew Whitehead/Alamy 31; Cover picture: Corbis

Every effort has been made to provide accurate information in this publication, but changes are inevitable. The publisher cannot be responsible for any resulting loss, inconvenience or injury.

Contact us

At Berlitz we strive to keep our guides as accurate and up to date as possible, but if you find anything that has changed, or if you have any suggestions on ways to improve this guide, then we would be delighted to hear from you.

Berlitz Publishing, PO Box 7910, London SE1 1WE, England.
email: berlitz@apaguide.co.uk
www.insightguides.com/berlitz

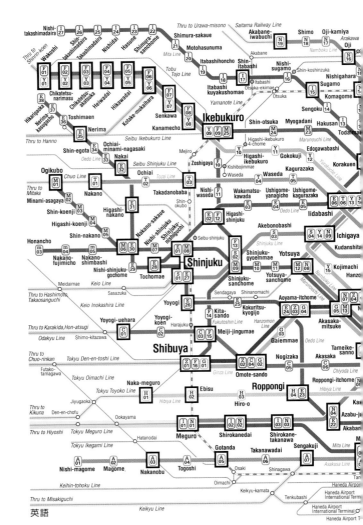

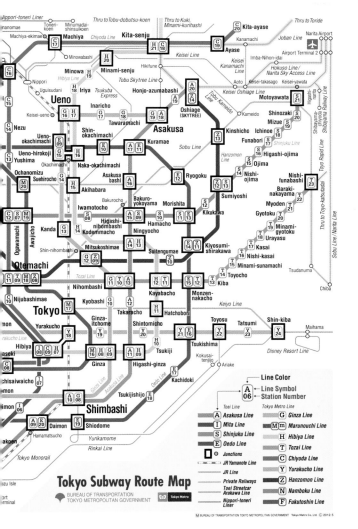

Tokyo Subway Route Map

BUREAU OF TRANSPORTATION
TOKYO METROPOLITAN GOVERNMENT

Tokyo Metro

Berlitz®

speaking your language

phrase book & dictionary
phrase book & CD

Available in: Arabic, Cantonese Chinese, Croatian, Czech, Danish, Dutch, English*, Finnish*, French, German, Greek, Hebrew*, Hindi, Hungarian*, Indonesian, Italian, Japanese, Korean, Latin American Spanish, Mandarin Chinese, Mexican Spanish, Norwegian, Polish, Portuguese, Romanian*, Russian, Spanish, Swedish, Thai, Turkish, Vietnamese
*Book only